How To Rethink The Future

Making Use of Strategic Foresight

Stephen Murgatroyd, PhD

CEO, Collaborative Media Group

Stephen Murgatroyd, PhD

How To Rethink the Future – Making Use of Strategic Foresight

ISBN: 978-1-329-13983-1

This Book is Dedicated To

All those who are passionately committed to their preferred future and to those whose daily work is dedicated to change, in particular:

Don Simpson, J-C Couture, Andy Hargreaves, Pasi Sahlberg, Dennis Shirley, Jean Stiles and the team at Jasper Place High School, Kate Lindsay, Connie Phillips, Carol Bettac, Ian de la Roche, Janet Tully, Areef Merali, Nadine Riopel, Dean DuPerron, many more...

and to all at The Collaborative Media Group.

CONTENTS

Preface

> *"But what ...is it good for?"* IBM Engineer commenting on the first microchip in
> *1968*
>
> *"Louis Pasteur's Theory of Germs is a ridiculous fiction!"* Professor Pierre Pachet,
> *Professor of Physiology at the University of Toulouse, reflecting the scientific
> consensus of the time, 1872*

We are not, as a species, very good at prediction. This you will quickly realize
as you read the first chapter of this book. Yet we need prediction to live our
daily lives – insurance, weather forecasting, shipping, flight and other decisions
depend on them. We make predictions all the time and sometimes we get it
right.

Strategic foresight is not about prediction. It is about understanding and
anticipating different futures. The future is rarely a straight line from the past –
it is subject to change and uncertainty. What strategic foresight as a process
does is seek to understand why the future will be different from the past and
what the implication of these differences are.

In this book, I provide insights from forty years of consulting practice with
organizations from large (Oracle, TESCO, Heinz, Barclays, Conoco-Phillips),
medium (Debenhams, West Yorkshire Police, Millennium Copthorne) and
small (Elk Island Public Schools, Alberta Assessment Consortium, Contact
North/Contact Nord); for-profit and non-profit; industry and professional
associations as well as charitable volunteer organizations. The focus of the
book is on how to undertake a strategic foresight expedition, including some of
the tools you will need to undertake this work (there is an Expedition Back
Pack and Tool Kit included) and how to connect this work to strategy.

The motivation for writing this book is simple: I wanted a single place where
the work I do is captured so that those with whom I work can see what the
work looks like.

I am not an "expert" on strategic foresight, but have been blessed to meet
several who were (including Herman Khan who I met and lunched with in
London and Stafford Beer who I spent time with in Cardiff) or are (Ruben
Nelson, Jeremy Heigh in Alberta as well as several members of the World
Future Society) and have worked on foresight projects for Canada's National

Research Council, the forest industry of Alberta and Contact North in Ontario. I have also published books which are foresight books (they are referenced from time to time in what follows).

The big learning is not in how to conduct strategic foresight exercises, but in how to connect this work to the task of building strategy and action plans. The real work lies in this connection.

I am grateful to all who helped me on this journey, especially to Don Simpson and Seth Goldenberg who show what foresight can do when coupled with compassion and commitment.

Stephen Murgatroyd, PhD FBPsS FRSA

CEO Collaborative Media Group

Canmore, Edmonton and Paris June 2015

Chapter 1: Prediction, Foresight and Risk

"I confess that in 1901, I said to my brother Orville that man would not fly for fifty years . . . Ever since, I have distrusted myself and avoided all predictions." – Wilbur Wright, 1908

"Prediction is very difficult, especially if it's about the future" – Yogi Berra

Introduction

People like to predict. Look at a typical edition of a newspaper and you will see predictions, whether it is about the weather, the economy, the future price of grain, a sporting event, the likely outcome of a trial – there are predictions everywhere. What is more, industries have been built around prediction – political opinion polling, gambling on horses or the outcome of soccer or cricket matches. Our life insurance industry is based on predictive models of life-expectancy and risk conditions. Millions are paid each day to "back" predictions and most of this money goes to the "bank" rather than the predictor - just visit Las Vegas.

Indeed, there are some systematic studies of our ability to predict which shows that we are not very good at it. Christina Fang, for example, offers evidence that the people who correctly predict extreme outcomes are, on average, bad predictors. She wanted to know about the people who make bold economic predictions that carry price tags in the many millions or even billions of dollars. Along with co-author Jerker Denrell, Fang gathered data from the *Wall Street Journal*'s Survey of Economic Forecasts to measure the success of these influential financial experts[1]. The takeaway: the big voices you hear making bold predictions are less trustworthy than the average person:

> *In the* Wall Street Journal *survey, if you look at the extreme outcomes, either extremely bad outcomes or extremely good outcomes, you see that those people who correctly predicted either extremely good or extremely bad outcomes, they're likely to have overall lower level of accuracy. In other words, they're doing poorer in general. … Our research suggests that for someone who has successfully predicted those events, we are going to predict that they are not likely to repeat their success very often. In other words, their overall capability is likely to be not as impressive as their apparent success seems to be.*

Others have found similar evidence of the inability of experts to predict near- and medium-term futures, never mind the long-term. For example, Phillip Tetlock author of *Expert Political Judgment*[2] and a Professor of Psychology at Penn State University provides strong empirical evidence for just how bad we are at predicting. He conducted a long-running experiment that asked nearly 300 political experts to make a variety of forecasts about dozens of countries around the world. After tracking the accuracy of about 80,000 predictions over the course of 20 years, Tetlock found:

> *That experts thought they knew more than they knew. That there was a systematic gap between subjective probabilities that experts were assigning to possible futures and the objective likelihoods of those futures materializing … With respect to how they did relative to, say, a baseline group of Berkeley undergraduates making predictions, they did somewhat better than that. How did they do relative to purely random guessing strategy? Well, they did a little bit better than that, but not as much as you might hope ….*

The psychologist Daniel Kahneman, who won the Nobel Prize in Economics for his work on decision-making, has looked at the issue of "experts" and why they often get things wrong. In his book *Thinking Fast and Slow*[3] he points to several aspects of their psychology as factors, but highlights two in particular: the illusion of understanding and the illusion of validity. These are primary causes of experts getting it wrong.

The illusion of understanding refers to the idea that the world is more knowable than it actually is. In particular, experts believe that they have an in-depth and insightful understanding of the past and this enables them to better understand the future. They use what Kahneman refers to as the WYSIATI rule – "what you see is all there is" and this provides the basis for their confidence.

For example, it *must be the case* that high levels of government indebtedness (levels of debt to GDP ratio above 90% is the most recent version of this[4]) stifle the economy and reduce investor and entrepreneurial confidence according to some notable economists. Or *it is obvious* that human generated C02 is the major cause of climate change according to some climatologists. Both of these understandings are based on a particular view of historical data and "facts" and an extrapolation of these views into the future.

The views exist independently of the evidence to support them. Just as financial advisers are confident that they are successful in predicting the future behaviour of stocks, so macro-economists are confident that their views of austerity have the weight of history behind them. Those committed to the view that human-produced CO_2 is the primary cause of climate change are not deterred by evidence that it may not be or that climate change has stalled for the last eighteen years, despite the continued rise of CO_2 emissions

Experts are sustained in their beliefs by a professional culture that supports them. Austerians (those who believe that austerity is the only way) have their own network of support, as do the Keynesians who oppose them. Anthroprocene climatologists who believe that man is the primary cause of global warming have their own network of support among climate change researchers and politicians while the skeptical climate scientists also have their support networks. All remain ignorant of their ignorance and are sustained in their belief systems by selected use of evidence and by the support of stalwarts. These supportive networks and environments help sustain the illusion of validity. It is an illusion because evidence which demonstrates contrary views to those of the "experts" are dismissed and denied – the expert position, whatever it may be is valid simply because they *are* expert.

Indeed, using Isaiah Berlin's 1953 work on Tolstoy (*The Hedgehog and the Fox*), Austerians and anthropocenes are "hedgehogs" – they know one big thing, they know what they know within a coherent framework, they bristle with impatience towards those who don't see things their way and they are exceptionally focused on their forecasts. For these experts a "failed prediction" is an issue of timing, the kind of evidence being adduced and so on – it is never due to the fact that their prediction is wrong. Austerians who look at the failure of their policies in Europe, for example, suggest that the austerity did not go far enough; anthroprocene climatologists see the lack of warming over the last eighteen years as proof that they are right, it is just that the timing is a little out.

Tetlock's work, cited above, is a powerful testimony to these two illusions – understanding and validity. His results are devastating for the notion of "the expert". According to Kahneman, "people who spend their time, and earn their living, studying a particular topic produce poorer predictions than dart throwing monkeys".

Tetlock observes that "experts in demand were more overconfident than those who eked our existences far from the limelight". We can see this in spades in both economics and climate change. James Hanson, recently retired from NASA and seen to be one of the world's leading anthroprocene climatologists, makes predictions and claims that cannot be supported by the evidence he himself collected and was responsible for. For example, he suggested that "in the last decade it's warmed only about a tenth of a degree as compared to about two tenths of a degree in the preceding decade" – a claim not supported by the data set which he was responsible for. This overconfidence and arrogance comes from being regarded as one of the leading climate scientists in the world – evidence is not as important as the claim or the person making it. Hanson would appear to suffer from the illusion of skill.

Kahneman recognizes people like Hansen. He suggests:

> ". overconfident professionals sincerely believe they have expertise, act as experts and look like experts. You will have to struggle to remind yourself that they may be in the grip of an illusion."

There are other psychological features of the expert that are worthy of reflection. For example, how "groupthink" starts to permeate a discipline such that those outside the group cannot be heard as rational or meaningful – they are referred to as "deniers" or "outsiders", reflecting the power of groupthink. The power of a group (they will claim consensus as if this ends scientific debate) to close ranks and limit the scope of conversation or act as gatekeepers for the conversation. Irving Janis documented the characteristics of groupthink in his 1982 study of policy disasters and fiascoes[5]. He suggests these features:

1. **Illusion of invulnerability** –Creates excessive optimism that encourages taking extreme risks. We can see this in the relentless pursuit of austerity throughout Europe.

2. **Collective rationalization** – Members discount warnings and do not reconsider their assumptions. We see this in relation to both climate change and austerity economics.

3. **Belief in inherent morality** – Members believe in the rightness of their cause and therefore ignore the ethical or moral consequences of their decisions. Austerians appear to willfully ignore the level of unemployment and the idea of a lost generation of youth workers,

especially in Greece and Spain. Anthropecene climate researchers generally present themselves as morally superior.

4. **Stereotyped views of out-groups** – Negative views of "enemy" make effective responses to conflict seem unnecessary. Climate "deniers" commonly face suggestions that they be prosecuted or punished in some way[6].

5. **Direct pressure on dissenters** – Members are under pressure not to express arguments against any of the group's views. This has occurred in climate change research community, since grants appear to favour those who adopt the view that man-made CO_2 is the primary cause of climate change.

6. **Self-censorship** – Doubts and deviations from the perceived group consensus are not expressed.

7. **Illusion of unanimity** – The majority view and judgments are assumed to be unanimous. This is especially the case in "consensus" (*sic*) climate change science and amongst austerians.

8. **Self-appointed 'mindguards'** – Members protect the group and the leader from information that is problematic or contradictory to the group's cohesiveness, view, and/or decisions.

– all of these characteristics can be seen to be in play in the two examples used throughout this chapter – economics of austerity and man-made global warming.

There is also the issue of the focusing illusion. Kahneman sums this up in a single statement: "nothing in life is as important as you think it is when you are thinking about it". "Government debt is the most important economic challenge facing society today" says a well known economist, or "climate change is a life and death issue" says US Secretary of State, John Kerry. Neither of these statements are true for anyone *unless* they are obsessive.

Society faces a great many challenges. Much will depend on our own preoccupations and what focus one takes for the concerns you have. Some are more concerned about the future of Manchester United or Chelsea football clubs than they are about debt, deficits or climate change. The illusion is that one person's focus is, by definition, better than another is simply because they are an expert in this field.

Nassim Taleb makes a very compelling argument against forecasting in several of his books, most notably in *The Black Swan*[7]. He explains that we can make use of very short-term guesses or predictions, but long-term forecasts are nothing more than pure guesswork. We are guilty of ascribing far too much predictability to the truly unpredictable. It is very common for our human brains to believe we are recognizing patterns that are only a random sequence of events. Experts have tried to overcome our human fallacies with tools such as quantitative modeling. However, even these models play only on our biases. We believe that models that have accurately predicted the future in the past are likely to predict the future going forward. But that is no more true than believing me when I tell you that a coin will land heads up just because I accurately predicted it would do so the last ten times.

Do We Really Need Predictions?

So if we are not very good at predictions, why do we keep on doing it? It is simple: we need predictions.

Let us look at five basic examples to see why we need to at least try to predict:

1. **Labour Supply** – when universities and colleges are funded to train nurses, teachers, doctors, dentists and engineers they do so on the basis of an anticipated demand for these professions. An under production of teachers or nurses will lead to significant challenges in the delivery of health care or education and while these professions are in high demand globally, the issue at the local State or Provincial level is, "will we have enough teachers and nurses for the foreseeable future?" Prediction is helpful in planning. The fact that we are not very good at prediction does not mean that we should not try.
2. **Crop Forecasts** – Farming is a tough business at the best of times. Crop forecasts are critical in helping farmers choose which crops to plant and for crop insurers to offer services to those farmers.
3. **Demographics** – City planners, transport planners, educational and health planners seek to understand demography so as to plan both capital and operational expenditure and investments. For example, The City of Lloydminster on the Alberta:Saskatchewan border is growing at 7% per year and all analysis suggests that this will continue for at

least a decade, due to the development of new oil and gas finds and a resurgence of oil field related activity in the region. How many new schools, ice rinks and recreational facilities, hospital beds and new roads / houses will be needed to serve a population that will double in fifteen years?

4. **Health Systems** – Health systems planners also look at both demography but at health trends and patterns. As they see childhood obesity increasing and this triggering diabetes and heart disease at a much younger age, they begin to plan facilities and services on the basis of anticipated need. They also invest in public education and promote policy decisions that may reduce the incidence of obesity, early onset diabetes and premature heart and stroke.

5. **Weather Forecasts** – are predictions that matter a great deal. If you are a sea captain of a fishing trawler you need both predictions and assessment of fish locations and weather systems forecasts to be able to make good decisions for the highest possible catch with the least risks to safety. If you run an airline, weather systems are critical in making routing decisions.

We could have listed more – predicting markets for product development and launch, predicting consumer and market behaviour for decisions about interest rates and quantitative easing, predicting birth dates for pregnant women. Prediction is important.

We work hard to improve our predictive ability. Take weather forecasting. There are still "glitches" – e.g. not predicting the scale of rain that leads to major floods, not predicting the exact path of hurricanes or major storms. But the accuracy of weather prediction over the last thirty years has improved dramatically. A recent and ongoing analysis of the accuracy of one, five and ten day forecasts in the US shows significantly improving accuracy of one day forecasts over the last decade (from 83% to 90%), ongoing improvement in both five and ten day forecasts and much better accuracy for storm and extreme weather events[8].

Predictions, Cautions and Risks

All predictions come with caveats. All statisticians make clear that they are making probabilistic statements – usually accompanied by some statement of the probability of their statements being correct. For example, political polling is usually accurate nineteen times out of twenty. Daily weather forecasts are accurate eighty seven times out of one hundred. Being clear that there is some uncertainty about a forecast or prediction is important.

Nate Silver, who not only accurately predicted both the scale of Obama's 2008 Presidential victory, but also did so for each state, predicted Obama's re-election when most other pollsters were saying either that it was too close to call or that Mitt Romney would win. Silver, a sports statistician who now works for Fox Sports, confidently predicted the Obama re-election and said that his table of forecast results was 75% accurate. In 2008, Silver correctly forecast 49 out of 50 state results and was within 0.9% of the popular vote and 21 electoral votes. He did it by creating probabilities using his weighting of the accuracy of polls.

Predicting the weather system for a near future carries lower risks from a predictive validity point of view that seeking to predict the climate in 2100. Predicting sea level rises in 2050 – said to threaten many small island states – is very difficult and contains a great deal of uncertainty. Yet some small islands have already not only made plans to evacuate and relocate, but have made the financial investments to do so. They calculate that the risks of the forecasts being wrong are less than the risk to the island and their people of the possibility that sea levels will rise. They have exercised what is known as the *"precautionary principle"*.

The Precautionary Principle
If the weather forecast for tomorrow says heavy showers throughout the day, we each plan to dress accordingly, carry an umbrella or rain gear and adjust our plans for the day to take into account the weather. We are applying the precautionary principle.

The sea captain who, on hearing the shipping forecast, decides to leave not on the next tide but later because the forecasts suggests that the sea and weather conditions will be "better" is exercising the precautionary principle. The fact that these forecasts are not 100% accurate is not the consideration – it is that they are "good enough" to determine action.

Many definitions of the precautionary principle exist. Precaution may be defined as "*caution in advance*," "*caution practiced in the context of uncertainty*," or "*informed prudence*". All of these definitions have two key elements:

1. **Anticipation**: an expression of a need by decision-makers to anticipate harm before it occurs. Within this element lies an implicit reversal of the onus of proof: under the precautionary principle it is the responsibility of an activity proponent to establish that the proposed activity will not (or is very unlikely to) result in significant harm;

2. **Obligation**: the establishment of an obligation, if the level of harm may be high, for action to prevent or minimize such harm even when the absence of scientific certainty makes it difficult to predict the likelihood of harm occurring, or the level of harm should it occur. The need for control measures increases with both the level of possible harm and the degree of uncertainty. So if a major volcanic eruption is said to be near at hand in, say, Naples then anticipatory evacuation is a better bet than seeing if we can improve the accuracy of the prediction.

The precautionary principle is in some ways an expansion of the English common law concept of 'duty of care' originating in the decisions of the Judge, Lord Esher, in the late 19th century. According to Lord Esher: "Whenever one person is by circumstances placed in such a position with regard to another that everyone of ordinary sense who did think, would at once recognize that if he did not use ordinary care and skill in his own conduct with regard to those circumstances, he would cause danger or injury to the person, or property of the other, a duty arises to use ordinary care and skill to avoid such danger." This statement clearly contains elements of foresight and responsibility, but does not refer to a lack of certainty, as the word "would" is used rather than "might", or "could". The other important difference is that the duty of care applies only to people and property, not to the environment.

We exercise the precautionary principle all of the time. In planning investments in new roads, housing, schools, health care facilities, we are responding to both current known needs and anticipated needs – overbuilding when capital and labour are "cheap" in anticipation of future demand and demographics. In environmental management, we cut fire lines through the forest to reduce the dangers of a forest fire, especially near residential areas.

The largest challenge in the invocation of the precautionary principle is the quality of the "evidence" which underpins the call to action. Climate change is a very good example of how a radical call to action to massively reduce CO_2 emissions is based on some questionable science which, in turn, has led to some questionable political and economic actions.

But the invocation of the precautionary principle – our key point here – occurs because predictions have been made which appear to demand action.

The Difference Between Prediction and Foresight

To this point we have focused on activities involving prediction – e.g. Obama will win a second term, predictions about the weather, predictions about demography – and their consequences, especially the invocation of the precautionary principle. We have observed that prediction is both probabilistic (Nate Silver was 75% confident in his prediction of the Obama re-election – he later revised his confidence level to 87.9%) and problematic and subject to a variety of cautions.

But is strategic foresight the same as a prediction?

No it is not. We have looked at prediction and the problems associated with it so as to position the idea that we need something *different from* prediction that helps us understand the future, especially if we wish to develop strategy. Being able to predict would be tremendous, but since we are so poor at it, we need to develop an approach that is both helpful, different and enables us to act.

What is Strategic Foresight?

Leaders, managers and those seeking to make critical decisions have traditionally relied on periodic and episodic information to make such decisions. Most decisions have been based on "gut feelings" about what worked in the past or use predictions that may or may not turn out to be correct. But, in the quickening cycles of change that we are experiencing now, foresight not hindsight is a more valuable managerial attribute.

Foresight comes through discovering and understanding changing landscapes through the use of real-time and historical structured and unstructured data. By analyzing far more information, using computers, knowledge management and specific methods, we can actually see the underlying trend patterns in complex data that signal far-reaching change far quicker than before. We can imagine the future by thinking about change in four dimensions:

- Examining and projecting current trends and issues
- Considering potential events or tipping points and "wild cards"
- Developing possible futures
- Choosing among the different futures available the most preferred future

Projecting current trends

Trends are changes that occur over varying time periods (usually medium- to long-term) in one or more of these major domains:

- **Political trends** – related to the ebb and flow of democracy, the key political issues that create opportunity and conflict, patterns of voter behaviour.
- **Economic trends** – patterns of economic activity, shifts in consumer behaviour, the emergence of new markets and the decline of established markets, patterns of public economy.
- **Technological trends** – emerging technologies and their impacts in specific fields (education, health, manufacturing, energy, travel and transportation, agriculture, etc.).
- **Social trends** – patterns of social behaviour and personal values which have an impact on both individual behaviour and community.
- **Environmental trends** – patterns of climate, ocean movement, species change and biodiversity, animal behaviour.
- **Legal trends** – patterns evident in law-making, law-enforcement and legal decision-making as well as in illegal behaviour.

Trends occur gradually but at varying degrees of speed and impact and, if both understood and anticipated, can be exploited to take advantage of the opportunity they suggest or to avoid the damage they may threaten. For example, anticipating correctly a technological trend such as the emergence and potential of the internet created many new global industries and transformed many established industries, but this trend is also spawning some undesirable effects which now need to be mitigated (identity theft, cyber-bullying, internet pornography accessible by young children).

Spotting the turning or inflection point before it happens is where the greatest opportunity to exploit the change often occurs. Crowds blindly pursuing a trend can often lead to the creation of a bubble (the 2008 US housing crisis, for example) with the result that, like lemmings, most go over the cliff together while those with more foresight who anticipated the bubble bursting (as several did) live to tell the tale.

Strategic foresight makes use of a range of methods including: (a) historical analysis of patterns and trends; (b) the use of "big data" analytics to understand current patterns and trends; (c) meta-analysis and scanning of research findings; (d) casual layered analysis – identifying the driving forces and worldviews underpinning diverse perspectives about the future and what it means to groups; (e) scenario planning – looking at all of the available analysis to discern several different interpretations of the future; (f) backcasting – working back from the future to the present and testing assumptions against data and established trends; (g) simulation – where a model of the future is built to simulate possibilities (e.g. climate change models); and (h) the development of future focused data rich games which enable "players" to experience aspects of the future. Many other methods are also in use, but these are the dominant components of the practice of strategic foresight.

Considering potential events

Trends are relatively easy to spot when a person or team has access to quality information and is skilled at knowledge management, but predicting the impact and likelihood of a likely future or bend in the trend is not. Unforeseen or uncertain events are hard to anticipate but we can learn from history and envision the type of surprise (a wild card in the extreme) that might come along. So asking challenging questions is as much a part of determining future success as finding the answers.

Considering possible events and setting future-based challenges helps to strengthen an organization at times of high potential change. For instance, Matsushita told his managers after the Second World War that he was artificially going to peg the yen against the dollar several multiples higher than it then was. He told his managers this new exchange rate would now be used to calculate his company's performance. His managers thought this was crazy and impossible to contemplate. When asked why he would do such a thing he pronounced, "because one day it will be at this level!" Several years later his scenario came true and Panasonic was able to flood the US market with cheap electronics and hence build an empire. Matsushita had prepared his company for the unthinkable and was ready when the tipping point came.

Today, several drink companies worldwide are preparing for a new unthinkable: the removal of all subsidies, and potentially the introduction of taxes, on the use of natural resources like water. They are preparing for the day when they will pay the true cost of using natural resources in their organizations, creating future competitive advantage and a more sustainable long-term strategy for their companies.

Considering potential events like tipping points and inflection points and surprises helps us to see how we might cope in a crisis or exploit the opportunity. It helps organizations become more resilient to change under more circumstances than just maintaining the status quo and hence increases the chances for survival, innovation, performance improvement, and long-term success.

Choosing among the options derived from foresight work

Like Matsushita's decision, choices have to be made from the considered trends and events and action plans put in place to maximize the outcomes and minimize the potential threats. Foresight activities therefore must be designed in such a way as to lead to action plans which lead to change. Using foresight without a plan to act on the outcomes is like buying all the ingredients for a creative meal, but never actually cooking.

Rarely do foresight activities lead to a single, clear and guaranteed pathway. Most lead to some critical choices which, taken together, represent a pathway to the future. Each choice can be based on a clear understanding of a pattern or trend – but that understanding itself has consequences. In physics, we have come to recognize that observing a phenomenon such as the behaviour of an atom can create change in the behaviour of that phenomenon – this is referred to as the Copenhagen interpretation in quantum mechanics. In foresight, we need to be careful to separate out our own "guesses" and biases from the work of conducting foresight. For example, if we seek to truly understand what is happening with respect to the economy, education, health care or climate change, we need to be mindful of our own biases and assumptions.

Conclusion

We have explored several themes in this chapter. In summary:

Prediction:

1. Prediction uses systematic methods to provide specific statements of what will happen.
2. Prediction relies on probability (levels of confidence in a prediction).
3. Predictions can be tested – they are either right or wrong.
4. The majority of predictions, including those by experts, are wrong.
5. Getting one prediction right (e.g. Nate Silver's prediction that Obama would win the 2008 election) is no guarantee that the same person making another prediction will get it right.
6. The use of prediction is widespread and necessary.
7. Continuous improvement is occurring so as to make prediction closer to what happens more often than not – e.g. improvements in short term weather forecasting.
8. Prediction leads some to invoke the precautionary principle – e.g. predictions concerning sea level rises have led some small island states to plan evacuations of entire countries and establish a new location for their population.

Strategic Foresight:

1. Strategic foresight seeks to understand patterns and trends in the medium to long term and generally does not make specific predictions.
2. Strategic foresight offers frameworks and pattern analysis to enable strategic decision-making.
3. Foresight uses a range of methods looking at historical data and patterns, current data and patterns and future focused review so as to develop frameworks for understanding patterns. Foresight requires the analysis of a range of data sources and evidence.
4. Foresight can be wrong – misunderstanding of patterns and trends – and be unduly affected by the observer's bias of those undertaking the foresight activity.
5. In general, the purpose of foresight is understanding a pattern or trend and its likely positive and negative impacts rather than prediction.

Chapter 2: Strategic Foresight in Action – The Steps in a Foresight Expedition

"The future does not just happen to us; we ourselves create it by what we do and what we fail to do. It is we who are making tomorrow what tomorrow will be. For that reason, futurists think not so much in terms of predicting the future, as in terms of trying to decide more wisely what we want the future to be."

Edward Cornish, President, World Future Society.

Introduction

Whenever you read about strategic foresight, the example of Royal Dutch Shell is cited as a classic example of why foresight matters.

In the early 1970s, Shell developed an approach to looking at the future of the energy sector, especially oil and gas. They wanted to be ready to exploit the trends that they saw. They used scenario planning in a major program of strategic foresight and developed metrics of each scenario so that they could track which of their key scenarios was showing that it was becoming dominant. One of their scenarios suggested that the Middle Eastern states rich in oil and working as the OPEC cartel would use their cartel power to change the price of oil such that it damaged the economies of the western political powers: the oil price would be used as a political weapon.

Few thought this scenario likely, but Shell began to see signs that this scenario was indeed emerging - they were tracking political and financial metrics that suggested that shifts were occurring. But Shell went further, in anticipation of this development, Shell diversified its investments in future oil production out of the Middle East, stockpiled oil supplies and ensured that its supply chains were not at risk. When the oil price suddenly increased (from $2.50 to $11 a barrel) in 1973, Shell was amongst the few organizations ready for the change, since its foresight had provided a basis for action. Noticeably, this foresight related to political trends not trends in energy. Oil prices rose in retaliation for the Western powers support of Israel in the Yom Kippur war in October 1973.

Others have benefited from foresight. In 1993, when the internet was in its infancy, several educational institutions used strategic foresight to map the future of online learning and saw significant opportunities, especially for mid-career graduate level learning. Athabasca University in Canada became the first university in the world to offer a fully online executive level MBA program in

1994. Now the largest program of its kind in Canada, the program took 64% of the executive entry MBA market in Canada by 1996 and is now ranked amongst the top 100 MBAs in the world. An independent study, by a major consulting company, of the market potential for this venture conducted in 1993 suggested that it would be a failure.

While the number of new cases of HIV and AIDS may be falling in sub-Saharan Africa, 1.8 million people were newly infected in this region in 2009 alone. The UN drew on Shell's approach to scenarios to devise three versions of the future that explored the consequences of different government actions. These scenarios helped to guide the leaders' response to the epidemic and to work out which response to the crisis would create the best outcome for Africa, Africans and the rest of the world by 2025.

These are examples of foresight leading to action which have proved positive for many involved. But there are some negative examples.

Spain used foresight to look at the future of its energy markets. It determined that it could significantly increase wind-power, help build a new market for wind technologies and create thousands of "green jobs" and at the same time reduce CO_2 emissions in line with the commitments made by the European Union. Its action plan required them to use subsidies to stimulate the growth of the wind economy but its scenario plan showed that this investment would quickly produce results. By 2012, Spain was home to the fourth largest wind energy system in the world.

However, their foresight assumptions were wrong. Spain now spends more money on wind subsidies (€8 billion) than it does on post-secondary education and training; has to import energy from other countries when the wind-doesn't blow (which is often); and has a massive level of unemployment. Many of its wind power companies have gone bankrupt and more will follow as Spain reduces and cancels subsidy programs. Similar developments are occurring in other jurisdictions. Spain's contribution to the mitigation of climate change is modest – its activities will delay temperature rises by 62 hours by the end of the 2030[9].

Spain looked at climate change and energy systems but did not look thoroughly at the global economic context and underestimated risks from other trends (e.g. the economic bubble). The result is that Spain was "caught" (as is Britain

16

and Germany) with energy strategies which will make it difficult for industry and domestic consumers to continue "business as usual".

What is Strategic Foresight?

This is the generally accepted definition of strategic foresight:

> *"the general ability to create and maintain a high quality, coherent and functional forward view, and to use insights arising* **in useful organizational ways"** *[our emphasis].*

The term strategic foresight has been in use for some time. It arises from the premise that: (a) the future is not predictable from simple review of current trends and patterns within an industry or economy – it is not a straight line from the present; (b) the future is not pre-determined; and (c) decisions we make today will influence future outcomes.

The work of strategic foresight is aimed at understanding adverse conditions, risks and uncertainties that should guide policy, shape strategy and explore the options for new products, services and markets. Rather than focusing on linear pathways from the present to the future, strategic foresight work looks at the future and casts back to the present, usually from a number of different scenarios.

Strategic foresight work is currently focused on 2030, 2050 and 2075, though some are working on slightly longer time frames (e.g. The Bi Puranen Institute for Future Studies, Stockholm or the International Panel on Climate Change). The key to understanding all of this work is that it uses a range of appropriate methods in a process that builds a community of interest that seeks a comprehensive understanding of an issue or set of issues so as to shape strategy and action. That is, strategic foresight is intended to make a difference to the current practices of organizations.

While there are many different approaches, the strategic foresight expedition or process is generally similar in shape. It involves several distinctive phases, a variety of methods and a strong and relentless focus on strategic action as the outcome of the work.

What Does a Strategic Foresight Expedition Look Like?

So how can we avoid the mistakes and challenges associated with prediction – the issues we explored in Chapter 1? What are the ground rules for the effective practice of foresight?

So as to understand the nature of strategic foresight and the ground rules associated with its practice, we use the metaphor of an expedition. Working on a strategic foresight project is an expedition – a journey – which has base camps, scouting parties, and summits.

Step 1: Preparing for the Foresight Expedition

To lead and support the strategic foresight expedition, leadership and key stakeholders must understand that a shared understanding of past and possible futures for the organization or system they are analyzing will catalyze more effective and aligned responses to issues in the present. It is the day-to-day decisions and enactments that ultimately shape an organization. The moves in this initial part of the expedition aim at involving a committed stakeholder's team in creating a clear process plan that engages the important parts of the organization in taking this special expedition. They might include:

- Listing crossroad issues which have led to the need for the expedition

- Sharing assumptions about the current state of the organization and the domains of patterns in which it operates – technology, demography, politics, environment, law, etc.

- Creating a design team to customize and guide the process

- Engaging top management in a clear sponsorship role

- Setting out basic ground rules for engaging in the expedition

These ground rules have to involve some basic conditions of engagement. In a recent foresight activity conducted with a major oil and gas company, the leadership team worked to establish these ground rules for their expedition:

1. **Respect**: All persons and their ideas, no matter how "whacky" they may appear, must be respected.
2. **Evidence Base**: No idea or observation is a bad one, provided there is evidence that can be used to support it.

3. **Understanding Why as well as What**: Assumptions are as important as observations and outcomes. We must therefore document both our observations and the assumptions which inform them in sharing with others.

4. **Our aim is to Understand**: this requires active listening. Talk less, listen more.

5. **Our aim is also to act Strategically**: the results of our listening, understanding and sharing must be tied to action that will enable this organization to prosper and be sustainable.

6. **Ideas not Status**: The idea leads, not the position of the person suggesting it.

Laying out these ground rules for dialogue and engagement made it possible for all engaged in the process – irrespective of status, time with company, gender or role – to know that their ideas and thinking mattered and would be taken into account. No one who had an understanding founded on evidence was to be excluded.

The important point here is that relating to assumptions. When we look at an issue – say the future of education – and see that there is a strong push to privatize public education on the grounds that "markets ensure quality" we need to document all of the assumptions behind this thinking and seek out evidence in support not just of the big proposition, but also for the assumptions behind it. When we do so we will often find that "the emperor has no clothes" – the big idea does not hold up when all of the assumptions behind it are subject to rigorous evaluation (see our discussion of predictions by experts in Chapter One).

From experience, the critical decision at this stage of the expedition is "who is in the room"? Too often executive teams fail to engage the organization's thought leaders and influencers in this work. Yet they shape the culture and experiences of the organization. Rarely do strategic insights come from just the executive leadership team. It is important to have thought leaders, influencers and those who can shape culture and know the context in the room.

Step 2: Current State Assessment: Exploring Context, History and Learning About the Current State

Having established ground rules and ensured that the right people are at the table, the expedition now moves up and back into history, engaging the intuition and feelings of participants by looking at the big picture.

Large scale group graphic techniques and large group gatherings support storytelling, acknowledgments, and release of the energy and learning tied up in past experience. This opening up is then grounded in more analytic exploration of core values, competencies, successes, and learning. Throughout this stage the group dialogues and documents its activities, always working in an exploratory mode, gathering a common base of respect and understanding for the strategic foresight journey ahead.

The key task is to understand the starting point. We have often used the McKinsey Seven S's for this work[10] – hooks on which to build the conversation. The 7S's are as follows – taken from work with a school district:

> **1. Structure**: an understanding of how a school, group of schools, a district or a jurisdiction is structured and organized in specific and sustained ways. What do we know about the strains and stresses in this structure and how is the structure being modified by the daily actions of the "players"?
>
> **2. Staff**: understanding the way in which staff are deployed or engaged in their work and the link between current deployment and school performance. The use of teaching assistants and specialists with respect to special needs is an example here of a changing landscape that needs to be understood.
>
> **3. Strategy**: being clear about the strategic intent of the organization and the link between strategy and sustained gains in outcomes.
>
> **4. Systems**: understanding the current state of business process innovations which significantly improve both efficiency and outcomes, such that the organization is seen to have made a significant performance improvement.
>
> **5. Style / Culture**: understanding the changes in the culture and style of the organization and their links to significant measurable changes in an aspect of the performance of the organization – the widespread use of problem-based learning and constructivist teaching may be an example here.

6. Shared values: what has happened over the last five to ten years to the strengthening of the shared values of the organization within a group of stakeholders or across more than one group of stakeholders which has lead to performance improvements?

7. Skills: understanding the current state of the skills within the system – the way in which each person in the organization demonstrates a high level of execution of the skills they possess and how the organization enables the continuous development of skills.

These seven domains of understanding enable us to focus on a conversation among our expedition members on the simple questions: (a) what has happened in the last decade which has had an impact on this domain?; and (b) what is the current state of the organization with respect to this domain?

Common methods used for this conversation at this stage of the expedition include (but are not limited to):

- Completing a Graphic History or a visual representation of the journey taken by the organization over the last decade or agreed time period.

- Identifying core competencies and historic values which are embedded together with an understanding of the current strengths and weaknesses associated with these core competencies.

- Creating a Context Map of the Relevant Environment – the internal and external factors which shape the organization "as is".

- Analyzing Industry Structure – the structure of the industry system of which this organization is a part. For example, in looking at a school district – what is the state of private provision for schooling and tutoring, competitive forces, competing demands for resources, people and time.

- Undertaking a timeline analysis of the critical incidents or "moments of truth" which have had an impact on the organization over the last 10-15 years.

Important in this work is visualization – representing the conversation in more than bullets and detailed notes. Being able to "see" the past in the present is important. In meetings and other group processes more and more organizations are using very large visual working displays, imagery and metaphor, and structured graphic templates to increase participation, productivity, and systems-level thinking in groups. Use of large scale, interactive visuals are limited by lack of training, availability of materials, and bias in some organizations against high participation processes. However, large scale graphics are uniquely suited for engaging groups in reviewing their organizational histories, surveying relevant environments, communicating visions and roadmaps. Such communications engage all forms of learning style.

Step 3: Finding Common Ground: Trends and Patterns
This stage in the expedition creates a solid platform of information and agreements which can serve as a springboard for foresight. It is also the starting point for a number of scouting parties – teams which look in depth at a particular issue or opportunity and report back.

When people know what some of the givens and boundaries are, they are freer to improvise and stretch. This seems paradoxical, but is a bit like standing in a doorway pressing your arms out, and then stepping free. Clarifying the understandings at this stage anchors and re-centers everyone in the present for a launch into foresight. It is very important to document these discussions, using such tools as group multi-voting and groupware to illustrate the extent of agreements.

We have also made extensive use of a process known as the Challenge Dialogue System (CDS) ™. This tool, developed by the Innovation Expedition, enables large numbers of people to explore the assumptions and implications and establish the degree of alignment they have with the boundaries and the assumptions behind them. For example, in a CDS on the future of Alberta's forests alignment was secured around a particular approach to stewardship based on a particular scientific framework (resilience plus natural disturbance science) and the evidence base associated with these frameworks. Alignment on these matters enabled significant and substantive change to be made in the approach to the management of the forest.

Useful approaches at this stage of the expedition, in addition to CDS, include:

- Agreeing on trends, assumptions, and imperatives at a basic level and then using scouting parties to explore the key trends in more depth.

- Analyzing strengths, problems, opportunities, and threats of the current organization using a SPOT[11] (strengths, problems, opportunities, threats) matrix or a SCORE[12] (strengths, challenges, options, responses, effectiveness) analysis.

- Identifying benchmarks and potential success models from a global review and then applying then to the local situation (going *glocal*).

- Interviewing customers, stakeholders and others for their perspectives and then uses these interviews to secure an understanding of trends and patterns in their response.

- Literature review of the future predictions about the industry or sector, being cautious about their value (see Chapter 1).

What is important is that a catalogue of key trends and assumptions is being built in a systematic way. Also key at this stage is that there is a developed agreement that the key trends being documented are worthy of in-depth consideration at the next stage – there is a development of a community of practice which is highly engaged in this work.

One tool we have made extensive use of at this stage is the development of a knowledge-bank or community information and resource centre. The Collaborative Media Group, for example, has been developing an online community of practice in which materials of any kind (video, audio, text, blogs, images) can be shared and stored in an interactive way (rather like facebook.com or linkedin.com) in a closed and secure space. Such a virtual collaborative tool truly enables the development of a sharing community and supports alignment.

Step 4: Opening Up to a Different Future – Developing Scenarios and Understanding Risk and Uncertainty

This step moves up and forward in the expedition, reversing the direction of attention from the last phase toward the future. The little rehearsals of thinking forward in the prior steps should have built a readiness to fly free with the group imagination. Indeed, one key task for those facilitating this process is not to get to the future too soon – the past and the present need to be fully understood and the trends leading to the future fully documented before the future can be approached.

The activities here should be tailored to the group and its readiness for different kinds of work. It is very important at this step of the expedition to leave evaluation behind, and open the group's collective arms to the voices of the intuition and deep feelings. Foresight and vision are most powerful if they represent real aspirations. They do not need to be worked out in every detail, but imagined powerfully and vividly. That is, there is a need to build ownership for: (a) the idea that the future is not a straight line from the past; (b) change is inevitable, but choosing how to change is optional; and (c) the future can be anticipated to some degree but not entirely – the group needs to learn with the discomfort of uncertainty.

Productive approaches for this step include:

- Conducting a vision retreat or search conference with a lateral slice of the organization aimed at building scenarios of the future, using the trends secured at the previous step and the visualizations of the past and the present at the second step. We explore scenario planning in more depth in Chapter 3 below.

- Using the Cover Story of a major magazine as a basis for an activity. This process features the group as the cover story in a major magazine imagined five or six years in the future. Major accomplishments are headlined, identifying the most compelling hopes and dreams for the organization. It is a way of backcasting.

- Exploring metaphors and stories that describe the future organization. What is happening in various parts of the organization 5, 10 and 15 years ahead?

- Creating a Futures Map or Visual which integrates information about the key elements of the future, values, critical issues, competencies, and major milestones.

The real challenge here is to use these kinds of methods not just to create energy or ideas, but to become more systematic. Futures thinking is easy. Being systematic and thorough is not.

The product of this step needs to be a statement of 2-4 alternative futures for the organization (each with their own names) and a decision about which of these futures is preferred. Knowing that not all elements which will lead to that future are under the control of those engaged in the expedition, a commitment to seeking to align energies and opportunities as well as actions to a preferred future is a powerful commitment for an organization to make.

Step 5: Creating Strategies Pathways to the Future – Getting to Strategy
Strategies link the learning from the past with the future by articulating a high level path forward. In a sense, they begin to bring the future and visioning back down to the ground.

Most organizations have no idea what strategy really is (Porter, 1996)[13]. They confuse strategy with operational planning or with tactical work. ***Strategy is a determined way for an organization to differentiate itself from others operating in the same space in a way that is sustainable over time***. Strategy is supported by activities and processes which are unique to that organization and which are bounded by simple rules (Eisenhardt & Sull, 2001)[14]. These rules relate to: (a) unique ways in which the organization functions – "how to" rules; (b) the way in which the organization defines the boundaries of its work – "boundary rules"; (c) what matters most in the organization – "priority rules"; (d) rules with respect to activities and time – "timing rules"; and (e) decisions about when the organization stops doing something – "exit rules".

Strategies should tell a powerful story of where to focus actions. Too many strategies and too complex strategies undermine their impact. For example, for many years the strategy for Scandinavian Airlines (SAS) was simple: be outstanding in the management of passenger's moments of truth. A moment of truth being those moments when the passenger feels their safety or experience is "on the line" as is the reputation of SAS. A lost bag, a late arrival, a missed connection are all reputational moments of truth for SAS. The foresight team realized if they could manage the 15-20 moments of truth for each passenger for each journey they would be running a world class airline which would be different from others – it would be relentlessly focused on passengers and the quality of their experience. That was the strategy adopted in 1982 under the leadership of Jan Carlzon. Within one year of adopting this strategy, SAS had become the most punctual airline in Europe and had started an on-going training program called *Putting People First*. The program was focused on delegating responsibility away from management and allowing customer-facing staff to make decisions to resolve any issues on the spot. Jan Carlzon said at the time: "*Problems are solved on the spot, as soon as they arise. No*

25

front-line employee has to wait for a supervisor's permission." These changes soon impacted the bottom-line as well and the company made a profit of $54 million in 1982. Several case studies about the turn-around are available and it has been referenced widely in management literature[15]. Following their success, others (especially Virgin Atlantic, Cathay Pacific, Qatar and Emirates) followed their lead.

The activities in this step of the process begin to integrate the work of the prior stages, so be prepared to bring forward documentation and charts. Re-post key templates, charts, maps, trend documents to create a room for whole systems thinking. We did this several times and called the room *The Imaginarium.*

Typical activities at this step include:

- Holding a Base Camp for all engaged in this process so that they can "own" the preferred future by collaborating on the design of that future.

- Conducting cascades of the implications of the preferred scenario, eliciting strategies that would deliver to this scenario.

- Identifying Five Bold Steps – actions which will lead to the future – so as to focus in on the critical steps needed to achieve a quantum shift in direction.

- Using future scenarios already developed and testing the strategies and bold actions against them.

- Using personal calling statements to connect the individuals engaged in this work with the strategy and bold steps associated with the strategy so that they know what they have to do to translate this thinking into personal action.

Step 6: Living the Future Now – Visualizing and Experiencing the Future
For strategic foresight expeditions to have impact they must be embraced by the larger organization and begin shaping the way systems and processes evolve in the organization. The most direct route is to involve as many people as possible in refining the preferred future scenario, strategies and five bold actions.

Another key part of this step is formal communications that let everyone know what is happening, and building feedback mechanisms. It's important during this phase to accept and honor resistance to changes. This is a sign of progress and the expedition having an impact.

Consider using such activities as:

- Having action teams create Graphic Game Plans for each key strategy.

- Using the expedition's work to focus key re-design projects aimed at critical areas – structural changes, business process changes and so on.

- Launching initiatives aimed at implementing key strategies and the five bold actions.

Stage 7: Living Your Vision In Action:

The ultimate success of a strategic foresight expedition is the extent to which leadership and key stakeholders actually begin living the preferred future they have chosen day-to-day.

If there is one thing that undermines a process of this sort, it is lack of genuine involvement and modeling of its significance. This is why key managers must be involved from the beginning, preferably leading the process.

It is even more crucial to demonstrate commitment to the new future and strategic plan when it is challenged by downturns or other "bumps" in the road. People in organizations know when their leaders are serious about things. "Be" the future to get real results.

Of importance here is:

- Integrating the preferred future and strategy into ongoing business planning and objective-setting processes.

- Developing measures of progress linked to a balanced scorecard which reflects the measured which would indicate whether the preferred future is coming to pass.

- Identifying and initiating critical "enactments" of commitments made in the strategic foresight process.

- Updating and using graphic visions as a major communications tool to underline the importance of the new directions and changes which arise.

Visualizing the Foresight Expedition

We have outlined the steps in a strategic foresight expedition and suggested tools and resources which can help with this work. So as to pull together some of this thinking and make it clear, we use a simple visual tool to represent the work. We provide this below, starting after the ground rules have been established (Step 1).

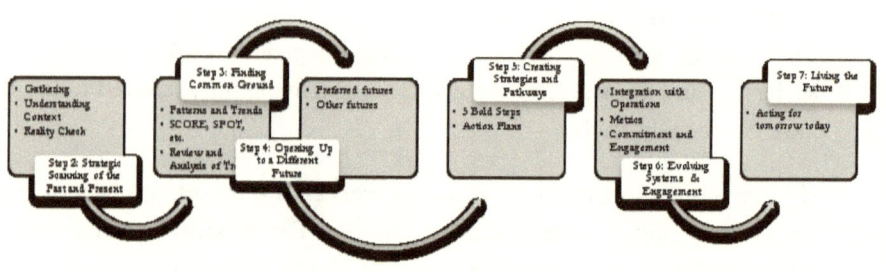

Figure 1: The Steps in a Foresight Expedition

Foresight should not be undertaken for foresight's sake. The intention is to make use of the insights and understanding developed through the process of strategic foresight to help influence, focus and direct current strategic action plans. Many foresight activities stop when the team feels it understands the 2050 or 2025 scenarios. The real challenge is to connect a systematic view of the future with present plans and activities and to maintain the tracking work on the emerging scenarios.

It is also important to maintain the relevance of *all* of the scenarios developed. Royal Dutch Shell, who we profiled at the beginning of this chapter, maintained systematic work on all of the key scenarios they had identified for

28

the future, including one that had a low probability. By doing so, they had in place a team who not only understood what was happening but had mapped consequences and responses for a five year period once the scenario began to play out. That is, they continued to work on all of the scenarios, even though they had identified their preferred scenario. When it became clear that other developments strongly favoured a scenario they had initially placed low on their list of possible futures, they were well equipped to work on plans to respond.

Thus, to be of value, it is clear that:

- Foresight needs to be embedded in the strategic and business planning exercises undertaken by an organization – it is part of what they do, not something "unusual" or "occasional".
- Foresight activities need to consider the spectrum of social, technological, environmental, economic and political factors that related to an area of work – e.g. if the focus is energy – foresight should not just look at the technological or scientific aspect of this work but at the social, environmental, political, economic and legal context.
- Although foresight can be facilitated by external consultants, it becomes really powerful when owned and used as part of the core business of the organization and is an ongoing process.
- Foresight activities should not divert attention from the core business of an organization, but should provide the context, vision, and purpose for those activities.

What Strategic Foresight Is Not

Many industry sectors and organizations have developed "roadmaps". The nature and scope of these vary. In some cases, such as the collection of energy roadmaps, they focus on a narrow area (e.g. Clean Coal or renewable energy) and see these domains largely in isolation from other technologies that could have a substantial impact on demand for coal or renewables and do not fully take into account socio-economic and political questions. That is, they are based upon a particular view of the future (not scenarios), come from a small group of experts (as opposed to a cross-functional Delphi or Challenge Dialogue System consultation) and make assumptions about parallel technologies or developments in other countries (for example, in this case, largely ignoring China).

In fact, energy is an area where, despite the best efforts of many, there is an abundance of strategic choices and an absence of foresight. Just in the period 2005-2009, the following "roadmaps" or strategy documents were developed:

- The Cleaner Hydrocarbons Technology Futures

- Clean Coal Roadmap

- Carbon Capture and Storage Roadmap

- Hydrogen Roadmap

- Oil Sands Roadmap. In addition to the above (that are themselves, just a sample of those available), there are a series of other current studies and initiatives:

- NRCan's *"National Energy S&T Strategy"*

- National Roundtable on the Environment and the Economy (NRTEE)

- The Energy Technology Working Group (ETWG)

- APEC Future Fuels Foresight Exercise (supported by the Canadian Office of the National Science Advisor)

- The Canadian Academy of Engineering's energy study: *"Pathways from Energy Sources to End Use"*

- National Dialogue on BioEnergy launched recently by BIOCAP and EnergyINet's Programs in Alternate and Renewable Energy

Without dismissing the relevance and intent of these roadmaps, studies and initiatives, they do not appear to adequately address long-term supply-demand energy options, taking full account of emerging technologies and disruptive technologies, the resulting technology requirements/barriers, and particularly the type of private:public partnerships and education needed to drive breakthrough innovations in a fully integrated way. What is more, they are not helping organizations focus on initiatives that will be in high demand 3-4 years from now, which is the focus of a great deal of technology commercialization activity. Foresight has to connect the future across sector boundaries (e.g. what impact will demographics have on energy systems and domestic demand for gas and electricity and how will these in turn impact?), across markets (what will India, China and Europe do with respect to carbon capture and storage?) and has to also look at alternative ways of understanding what may occur – hence the focus on scenarios.

Foresight also has to look at and anticipate the likely impact of disruptive technologies on current market assumptions, firms and industries. Foresight is thus more than trend analysis and "insular" industry road-mapping. As one observer has commented, "we have so many roadmaps, what we really need now is an atlas!" What he might have said, and this is the key point here, is that roadmaps are only helpful if you have a preferred destination.

Conclusion

This work is important. A study by the UK's Institute of Directors (UK) in 2006 found that most companies (94%) thought that a systematic approach to understanding the future would be very valuable to the organization, but only a few (16%) actually took the time to understand the future and its implications (positive and negative) for them. The resultant lack of use of strategic foresight has had many consequences for the organizations that did not use this approach, as the 2007-8 meltdown of the global economy shows.

Chapter 3: Setting the Ground Rules and Defining Scope

Introduction

When we begin a foresight expedition the critical first task is to assemble the right team. Who is recruited for this expedition is a critical challenge for those who have decided to undertake it. Who is on the team will determine what comes out of the team.

Commonly, those in senior leadership positions undertake this work. While this is understandable – strategic direction is, after all, a responsibility they have – it is not always the right group to undertake foresight work. There are five reasons for this:

- Many of those in senior leadership positions "own" the current ways in which the organization / system operates. They may be hesitant to cast it aside during the expedition to look at the "new".
- Each of the leaders in the organization are focused on specific roles and functions, not on "systems" and "trends" coming from outside which will have an impact on the organization / system *as a whole*. They will be inclined (from experience) to defend "their turf" rather than be open to looking at the organization as a system – as a whole.
- Just focusing on senior positional views minimizes the experience and wisdom of those nearest to the "customer" or "client" and of those new to the organization, who often have significant insights.
- Focusing solely on internal leaders minimizes the value of external stakeholders – e.g. suppliers, logistics services, industry analysts – who can also offer valuable insights.
- Senior leaders, especially those facing challenges of succession, will often use foresight and strategic processes to position themselves (as opposed to the organization) for the future.

Powerful foresight activities need to involve those who can contribute most to the process and over the course of the process, the more who are engaged the more ownership and commitment can be built to the future.

Who Should be On the Foresight Team?

Champions
The ideal team needs to have champions who support and will participate in the work. These must include senior leaders of the organization or system looking at its future as well as those who determine strategy resulting from this work.

Champions oversee the foresight expedition, provide advice and assistance on critical issues and champion the foresight work at every opportunity they can. They are engaged at a strategic level, not necessarily in all activities and certainly not in the management of the expedition. Champions represent the purpose of the foresight expedition and are attached but not directly engaged in all of the activities.

Outfitters
The expedition team needs a small, focused active and engaged group who manages the foresight process and stewards the engagement of others. They make sure documents are available on time, that others who need to be engaged at different stages are engaged, they make sure the outcomes of the expedition at each stage are communicated and they steer the expedition's journey.

Expedition Members
At various stages of the expedition, different people need to be engaged and involved. For example:

Step in the Foresight Expedition	Who Might Be Involved
Step 1: Start Up	Champions, Outfitters
Step 2: Looking at Current State	A cross-section of managers, supervisors, customers, industry analysts, supply chain members and critics.
Step 3: Finding Common Ground – Looking at Trends and Patterns	A cross-section of executives, managers, supervisors, customer-facing workers, customers, stakeholders, industry analysts, critics,

	journalists.
Step 4: Opening Up to a Different Future - Building Scenarios	A small team from amongst those engaged + champions.
Step 5: Understanding Risk and Uncertainty	A small team from amongst those engaged + champions.
Step 6: Getting to Strategy	A small team from amongst those engaged who then engage the widest possible group of colleagues through a challenge dialogue process. Working on visualization also requires a creative team.
Step 7: Getting to Action	Turning from strategy to action plan brings foresight back into the organization – normal line functions should take strategy and turn it into action plans with measurable accountability.

Engagement

The expedition should be designed to involve as many people as possible within the organization over the course of the journey: not all have to be engaged at every stage, but if the intent of the journey is to equip the organization for a changing future so that it is relentlessly focused on doing the right thing at the right time for the right reason and to be nimble in response to change, then all need to understand not just what they need to do but why.

Establishing the Ground Rules: The Expedition Charter

Some of the great expeditions of our time – Hilary's ascent of Everest, the first man on the moon – all began with what is known as a "focus and alignment" activity. That is, those most engaged in the journey spent time understanding the "rules of the game".

An expedition charter – a team charter if you like – is something that Champions and Outfitters need to develop, own and commit to. A typical team charter (see the Expedition Back Pack and Tool Kit at the end of this book) has these elements:

- Our purpose and commitment to each other
- Our values
- Our way of working
- When conflict arises we will…
- When we conclude our work we will …

In Chapter 2 we outlined some key statements which should inform all aspects of this work. It is worth repeating these here:

1. **Respect**: All persons and their ideas, no matter how "whacky" they may appear, must be respected.
2. **Evidence Base**: No idea or observation is a bad one, provided there is evidence that can be used to support it.
3. **Understanding Why as well as What**: Assumptions are as important as observations and outcomes. We must therefore document both our observations and the assumptions which inform them in sharing with others.
4. **Our aim is to understand** – this requires active listening. Talk less, listen more.
5. **Our aim is also to act strategically** – the results of our listening, understanding and sharing must be tied to action that will enable this organization to prosper and be sustainable.
6. **Ideas not Status**: The idea leads, not the position of the person suggesting it.

The implicit behaviours here are: respectful behaviour towards others, integrity in all that is said and done, active listening, caring for others and their ideas, challenging an idea not the person suggesting it and making sure that status isn't get in the way of the work.

A Map of the Expedition – What will the Journey Look Like?

It is always helpful to use maps to show where the foresight expedition is going. Visual maps – showing a road to be followed (including mountains to be climbed, turbulent waters to be crossed and bridges to be built) over time help expedition members and those following the work of the expedition understand what the journey will look like.

The team should get used to presenting its ideas and its work in more formats than just a written document. Many individuals are visual learners – they use images and visual resources to help understand and master a skill, body of knowledge or an understanding. Use many different media to present ideas and information. Maps are just one format.

Defining Scope –What's In and Out of the Expedition?

A key challenge in all foresight work is to identify the boundaries of the work: what is in scope and what is out of scope?

In a recent consultation on the future of Alberta's bioeconomy, for example, a key challenge was to determine whether all bio products and services were to be included, even though some were marginal (neutraceuticals and cosmetics, for example) and some were not industrial (eco systems services, for example). In our work on the future of the forest industry, did we just focus on the current range of products (pulp, paper, logs, finished wood for construction, engineered wood products) or look at the full range of possible products from the forest (pharmaceuticals, food additive, methane, ethane, etc.)?

The approach taken in both cases is to define what is absolutely to be included, what sits close to this and what is out of scope? It is also important to do this at the start of the work, rather than the end – it will save a lot of time. As a strategic foresight expedition begins its journey, items that were "sitting close" to the core suddenly become central to the future. For example, bioenergy and biochemical are central to the future of pulp mills in certain jurisdictions under certain conditions. This may or may not have been evident at the start of a strategic foresight journey.

Conclusion

Set-up and start-up often determines where you will end up. If the expedition starts from the wrong place it will not end up in the right place.

This is an important step and needs very careful thought. The wrong team working on foresight, as has happened in many organizations, can kill the exercise before it starts. Make sure that critical voices are engaged from the get go and also make sure that there is a clear map not simply of the kick-off but how the journey will continue.

Chapter 4: Current State Assessment

"You can't get to where you want to be by remaining where you are."

"I'll be more enthusiastic about encouraging thinking outside the box when there's evidence of any thinking going on inside it." — Terry Pratchett

Introduction

When we began work on a current state assessment of the forest sector in Alberta, everyone engaged thought they knew clearly where they were and what the "lay of the land" looked like. They were wrong. Those directly engaged day-to-day in the industry were unaware of some of the conditions that were evident in the global market for the goods and services, some of the regulatory conditions of their current state and some of the forces operating on their industry. Just because you make it work every day, does not mean that you fully understand just how and why it is working every day and what works only occasionally.

Scanning the Present for an Organization

Most scanning activities undertaken today focus on the past and the present. The key questions being asked are: *"where are we?"* and *"how did we get here?"*

Michael Porter developed a systematic approach to these questions in his book on *Competitive Strategy*[16]. It essentially involves looking at an organization, like a firm, industry, school system, nonprofit organization, profession or network organization and exploring these questions (we use the example of a school system – see the questions as samples rather than a comprehensive questionnaire):

The Core Operation

- **What are the outcomes of our current activities –** educational achievements, social outcomes, community outcomes?
- **What are the internal conditions of the school system –** staff morale, staff turnover (recruitment and retention), student recruitment and retention, building condition (repairs and maintenance), management: union issues and conflicts, parent and student engagement and satisfaction, teacher satisfaction?

- **What are the costs of the operation and what does the historic cost model look like** – how sustainable is the current system on the basis of current models of funding and student enrollment / staff costs?

The Supply Chain Environment

- **Supply of People**: How sustainable is our core supply chain? Will the demand for our services from parents continue? Will our ability to attract and retain teachers remain the same? Will our ability to support students with special needs keep up with demand?
- **Supply of Materials**: Do our technology and materials supplies meet our needs and will they continue to do so?
- **Transport and Logistics**: How successful is our current ability to transport students to and from the school? Is our current system on student transport sustainable?

External Factors Impacting the Operation

- **Competition**: What are our competitors doing? What impact is it having on our operation? Is there a threat of substitution (e.g. tutoring, online learning)?
- **Stakeholders**: What are our stakeholders saying about us? Parents, community organizations, feeder schools / receiving institutions?
- **Technology**: What impact is changing technology having on our organization?
- **Demographics**: What impact is demography having on our organization?
- **Media**: What impact do the media have on our organization (if any)?

These questions (or versions of them) can be adapted and used by any organization looking in a systematic way at their current situation. The aim is not simply to develop lists of responses, but to use these questions as a basis for an analysis of what the current state is.

The Current State of a Jurisdiction

Some time ago my colleague, Jeremy Heigh (President and CEO of *Sift Everything*), developed a systematic approach to understanding the current state of a jurisdiction – a region, a City, a State or Province, a nation. He suggested that there were a number of domains of the current state that need to be understood. These included:

Capabilities

- What are the unique technologies, skills and abilities within the jurisdiction which others would find difficult to replicate and deploy?
- Are there supply chains and logistics available in this jurisdiction which reflects unique capabilities which are not easily available elsewhere?
- Are there systems for skills development and life-long learning which support specific competencies and skills which are needed to support the capabilities of the jurisdiction?

Supporting Institutions

- Does the jurisdiction have universities, colleges and specialist institutions which contribute to the unique skills and abilities of the jurisdiction?
- Are there other supportive institutions unique to the jurisdiction which helps to sustain jurisdictional capabilities – e.g. industry associations, cluster organizations, unique R&D facilities, etc.?

Constructed Environment

- Is there a government policy / regulatory regime which is enabling of local industry and competitive advantage?
- Are labour regulations and policies aligned with the need of the sector(s) in which competitive advantage is sought?
- Is the infrastructure (roads, bridges, waterways, distribution and logistics) aligned with the needs of the sector(s) in which competitive advantage is sought?

Natural Environment

- Do the environmental conditions – water, natural resources, air quality, access to forests and agricultural products – meet the needs of the sector(s) in which competitive advantage is sought?
- Are there natural resource constraints to the growth and sustainability of the sector(s) in which competitive advantage is sought?

Sector Eco-System

- Is the balance within the sector(s) in which jurisdictional advantage is sought right between co-operation and competition?
- Do those seeking jurisdictional advantage have access to the right people, sources of venture capital, market intelligence and labour resources needed to sustain and grow the sector?

– this is not a comprehensive list of questions developed by *Sift Everything* (nor are the metrics they developed available here), but they do represent the kind of questions and domains of understanding needed to scan the environment for a current state assessment linked to jurisdictional advantage.

The point of these two examples is simple. Whether one is looking at the current state of a school system or of a jurisdiction which is seeking to gain competitive advantage, there is a need for a rigorous approach to scanning.

Scanning Methods

There are a variety of tools which can help this stage of the work of strategic foresight. Some of the more common ones are:

- **Using a SWOT analysis**: Evidence is collected (not just opinion) on the current strengths, weaknesses, opportunities and threats facing the organization or industry or system. The strengths of this approach when done well are that it provides a framework for looking at both underlying conditions and at the emerging issues. The challenge is that a lot of what passes for SWOT analysis is in fact SWOT opinion – it is rarely done well. What is required for success is to demand evidence and a rationale for each item included in each part of the SWOT.

- **Using SCORE analysis**. A variation of SWOT is known as SCORE (strengths, challenges, options, responses and effectiveness). This is a more rigorous and mindful approach to current state analysis than SWOT for two reasons. First, it looks at different thought processes (options, effectiveness and responses for example), requiring linking elements of the analysis together. For example, in identifying a challenge (e.g. demography in the case of schools) there is a need to look at responses and the effectiveness of these responses. Second, from the get-go this approach has been an evidence-based approach. While some opinions find their way into the SCORE process, they have to be linked to evidence and analysis.

- **Benchmarking** – a great many organizations look at themselves without systematically looking at benchmarking data. For example, universities who claim to be pursuing a strategy of being "in the top 10 by 2020" don't systematically look at where they really are at the start of this journey using rigorous benchmarking data. Companies who want to be "market leaders" need to understand both the markets they want to be leaders in (by segment) and where they really are at this time.

- **Undertaking a Baldrige Assessment** – The Baldrige Awards are a statement of quality in terms of all aspects of how an organization operates. The Awards are based on a set of assessments of the organization undertaken both as self-assessments and by an external panel of reviewers. The focus of the assessment process is on leadership and governance, finance and markets, products and processes, customers and the workforce. The criteria are adaptable rather than prescriptive – there are in fact a version for non-profit, education and health – and enable an organization to systematically look at itself through the mirror of established criteria and benchmarks. The self-assessment process will give a very strong view of the current state of the organization. It will not, however, look at all of the external forces which impact the organization.

- **Stakeholder Panels and Workshops Using Six Thinking Hats** – Using meetings of a cross-section of stakeholders to undertake an analysis of the current state using Edward de Bono's *Six Thinking Hats[17]*. The question is, *"What is the Current State of <insert the organization, industry, system etc.>?"* Then one proceeds through the Black Hat (all the cautions about the organization), Red Hat (all of the emotions associated with the organization), Green Hat (all the possibilities latent within the organization), White Hat (all the facts and key pieces of information about the organization that are pertinent to the question), Yellow Hat (all the optimism and positives). If you're counting, the sixth hat is the Blue Hat and is the controlling hat – used for managing this process.

- **Gap Analysis. One process used a lot is to look at the** difference between what the organization says it will do and what it actually does. For example, if a school system makes *claims about the* way it supports stu*dents with special needs; does it do what it says it will do? If a Government co*mmits to a certain class-size in schools, what does the data tell us about what is happening on the ground? Once differences have been found between commitments and reality, there is then a need to understand why these gaps occur. **Maturity Assessments. In organizations that have adopted Six Sigma** as an approach to continuous improvement and quality, there is a Six Sigma process known as a "Maturity Asses*sment". The or*ganization reviews *itself (assess), analyzes the results and then seeks to address the concerns the review* has revealed. This is why this process is known as the 3A Maturity Approach – Assess / Analyze / Address. There are various versions of this online, but we prefer a very basic approach[18] which uses rating scales.

- **Desk Review** of all the information (evaluation studies, reports, accounts, assessments of the organization) which helps us understand the current state.

Pulling the Scan Together

The challenge with this work is that there is a lot of material at the end of it. How does one make sense of it all? In one foresight study of the Alberta Forest Industry the slide-deck of the current state of each sector of the industry comprised in total of over four hundred slides packed full of information and analysis. Few could make use of it.

From experience, there is a need to keep it simple. Several methods can support this:

1. **Use logic models to capture the current state**. Logic models are in extensive use in a variety of organizations; especially those using results based management (RBM). So as to understand the results (outcomes and impacts) sought, there is a need to understand the logic of the activities which will lead to these results. Logic models are usually presented on a single piece of paper (usually legal size) and have these columns:
   a. What are the drivers which impact the organization? These are the primary challenges the organization is responding to.
   b. What are the primary resources the organization is utilizing in responding to these drivers?
   c. What are the core activities of the organization – the ones that matter in producing outcomes?
   d. What are the core outcomes of the work of the organization – the ones that matter most?
   e. What are the impacts of the outcomes of the organization – the reputational basis for the organization?

   An example of a logic model is given at the end of this chapter (it is an abbreviated one).

2. **Use outcome maps to capture the current state**. Outcome maps are different from logic models – they seek to build a picture of the activities of the organization that lead to outcomes. For example, a low cost airline achieves low cost by: (a) using online booking systems; (b) no seat allocations – first come first served; (c) restricting carry-on baggage to a single item – no overhead baggage storage which then speeds passenger loading; and (d) fast turnaround of aircraft between arrival and departure – and so on. An outcome map maps the activities, key components against outcomes. For scanning purposes, well executed activities can be colored green, those that are problematic, amber and those that are failing, red. This gives a picture of part of the current state.

3. **Use stories to capture the essence of the current state**. Story telling is a powerful way of making clear what the current state of play looks like. Stories make current state assessment come to life. For

45

example, contrasting a wealthy private school with a poor inner-urban school and showing the two side by side and telling stories (using video, audio or other images as well as narrative) makes a powerful case about inequity in the school system. You can see such a story – that of Periscope the "app" by following our reference[19].

4. **Use visualization to capture the current state**. Powerful and simple graphic representations can capture current state assessments well. Many such visualizations exist (for example, see our reference[20]) and are increasingly used for this purpose.

5. **Use Five Big Themes** to summarize the analysis of the current state. Imagine you have five Power Point slides, each of which can carry a single message about the current state of the organization, industry or system you are reviewing. What would each slide say? What would your conclusion be? You can always back each slide up with a document or a more comprehensive slide deck.

Conclusion

The point of scanning is to understand, warts and all, the current state and to use this analysis to position the challenges faced by the organization. The working assumption is that, "if we continue to do what we always do, we will get different results" given that the world is changing around us. Ask Nokia, Blockbuster, HMV, Woolworth, Virgin Records and many others who are no longer with us.

Appendix to Chapter 4: Logic Model

The following logic model was developed for the Government of Ontario and sought to show on a single page how all of the activities of the Government across different Ministries were a response to the climate change challenge. It enabled the Government to ask the question, "what is the current state of our response to climate change?"

This is a condensed logic model. Others are much more elaborate. You can see examples in the Logic Model Workbook, which can be found at http://www.innonet.org/client_docs/File/logic_model_workbook.pdf

INTEGRATED, FOCUSED PROGRAM	LEAD TO THESE OUTCOMES AT	LEAD TO PROSPERIY STRETEGY
PRIMARY INPUTS	KEY PROGRAM OUTCOMES	KEY LONG-TERM OUTCOMES FROM INTEGRATED STRATEGIES
CLIMATE CHANGE / CLEAN AIR	CLIMATE CHANGE / CLEAN AIR	SOCIO - ECONOMIC
· **Regulatory Framework**	· Low carbon, prosperous economy over the short, medium and long term	· Continued economic growth through a more diversified economy
· **Incentives and capital allowances**	· Reduction of GHg to near Kyoto levels	· Good for jobs over the long term – enhancing the skills and flexibility of the workforce
· **Preferential purchasing**	· Growth of new green technology industry with export focus	· Attract, Retain and Grow Companies
· **Public education and awareness**	· Smog reduction	· Encourage, enable and engage companies in the development of new technologies for value added activities
BIOECONOMY STRATEGY	· Efficient integration of renewable and non renewable energy sources	· Excellence in selected areas for Ontario's diversified economic future – Ontario as a global leader in defined sectors
· **Regulatory review**	· Highly educated and climate responsible population	· More efficient, sustainable and competitively priced energy supply

• Setting standards	**BIOECONOMY STRATEGY**	• Sustainab le communities
• Focused R&D and commercialization	• Greater % of energy from local renewable resources – utilizing current "waste"	• Support for northern and rural communities
• Industry partnership	• Improved competitive position of the bisector throughout the economic value chain	**ENVIRONMENT / QUALITY of LIFE**
ENERGY	• Lowered toxicity of products and processes – reduced CO2 emissions	• Ontario a Global Leader in Effective Climate Change Responsiveness – Strategic and Adaptive
• Clean energy to replace coal fired energy sources	• Energy efficiency	• Sustainab le environment and clean air
• Enhance overall capacity	**ENERGY STRATEGY**	• Reduced waste of natural resources
• Support green energy technologies and lead in their implementation & export	• Integrated power system plan	• Better balance between renewable and non-renewable sources in the energy supply chain
• Aggressively pursue energy conservation	• Clean energy displacing polluting energy	• Quality of life continuously improving
	• Conservation culture	
MANUFACTURING STRATEGY	• Green technology development, adoption and export	
• Support for new innovations in product s and processes	**MANUFACTURING STRATEGY**	
• Investment in energy efficiency	• Innovative investments to support competitiveness and productivity gains	
• Investment in waste reduction	• Lowering energy consumption and reducing waste	
• Industry partnerships	• Accelerating adoption of "game" changing technologies and business processes	
FOREST SECTOR STRATEGY	**FOREST STRATEGY**	

· Loan guarantee and selected co-investment in innovation, energy efficiency and waste reduction	Consolidate industry where appropriate and encourage/enable growth of
· Public:Private partnership initiatives	· secondary industries
· Focused R&D investments	· Lower energy consumption and encourage adoption of new technologies
· Regulatory review	· Reduce waste
INNOVATION STRATEGY	**INNOVATION STRATEGY**
· Continued support for research	· Support the attraction, development, growth and retention of companies through support for innovation and research
· Investment in early stage capital	· Leverage strengths in existing infrastructure to improve productivity, competitiveness and exports through early adoption of new technologies and through the adoption of best practices
· Development of skills for highly qualified people	· Stimulate and help to foster a strong culture of commerce and an economy attractive to business
· Targeted investment in R&D	· Develop an adaptive workforce with strong skills – ready to embrace innovation opportunities
· Extracting value from research	· Strengthen the innovative capacity of Ontario

Chapter 5: Patterns, Trends and Wild Cards

"Coming back to where you started is not the same as never leaving." — *Terry Pratchett, A Hat Full of Sky*

Introduction

In the book, *Rethinking the Future – Six Patterns Shaping the New Renaissance*[21] I outlined six major trends which are changing the way in which we live and work and build community. I chose the six on the basis of compelling evidence that these were the primary drivers of change in the developed world. These were:

- Demography
- The Global Economy and Austerity
- Weakening of Global Institutions and Shifting Power Balances in the World
- Changing Environmental Conditions, Most Especially Water
- Technology
- Individual Identity

This is not the place to represent this analysis and the implications drawn, but they are examples of trends or patterns which are having an impact on a variety of organizations and communities.

Shortly after *Rethinking the Future* was published, Al Gore also published a foresight text. *The Future – Six Drivers of Global Change* [22] looked at another list of six drivers. This is his list:

- Earth Inc. and the exploitation of natural resources and the challenge of population growth – how we need to respond to the fact of 10 billion people on a planet "designed" for 2 billion (according to Gore).
- The Global Mind – the growing globalization of everything.
- Power in the Balance – shifts in global power.
- Outgrowth – the rate at which society is outgrowing its capacities.

- The Reinvention of Life and Death – changes in demography and health and new developments in stem cell research which may make available much longer life spans.

- The edge – climate change and challenges to our natural environment are placing man at the edge of catastrophe and yet we demonstrate an inability to effectively respond.

For Al Gore, the first "green" billionaire, these are the patterns and trends he wishes us to look at since they shape the scenarios he wishes us to explore.

While there are overlaps between these two recent books looking at trends and patterns, the point is that both use a great deal of evidence-based materials to put a case for the trends and patterns identified to be seen as part of an account of the drivers of the future. A key task at this stage of any foresight expedition is to undertake the search for such relevant patterns and trends.

A Trend or a Pattern?

Before we describe how we look for trends and patterns, we should take a moment and understand what a trend is and how it differs from a pattern.

The word *trend* is used with a variety of meanings. The meaning relevant to strategic foresight is that of a regular change in data over time – for example, people talk about upward trends in the stock market or in the consumer price index. In research, the rules for inferring a trend from data are a bit more rigorous than those used in other fields. Four rules in particular should inform our thinking.

First, a trend cannot be inferred from two points. For example, if the crime rate drops from one year to the next, that's not evidence of a downward trend in the crime rate. It's unlikely the crime rate is going to be exactly the same from one year to the next. For example, if the crime rate is steady the probability of some drop in it from one year to the next is still effectively 50%. A change in the crime rate is therefore not in and of itself evidence of a trend.

Second, you cannot pick convenient spots for your trend to begin and end. People sometimes will observe that the crime rate has increased, say, for three or four years in a row, and decide that that's a trend. However, since they picked only years when the rate was increasing the main conclusion you can draw is that they're "sandbagging".

Similarly, you cannot simply draw a line between the first data point in your series and the last and call that your trend. Any measure includes error, so it is not a completely accurate measure of the variable whose trend you're interested in. You have to fit a trend line with a statistical technique to get a legitimate estimate of the trend.

Finally, no change is a trend until a statistical test says it is. Statistical tests evaluate the likelihood of changes happening and they can tell you pretty quickly whether or not a change is likely to be consistent over time. They also give you a pretty good idea of how strong the trend is. The statistical techniques to use are founded on statistical correlation, and include regression analysis and multidimensional scaling. Multiple linear regression offers the advantage of being able to separate the effects of elapsed time from other effects correlated with elapsed time.

In contrast, a **pattern** can be thought of as a model or archetype. For example, if flooding in a particular area always follows the same path (certain areas are affected and not others), then we can say that the flood pattern is described in a particular way – areas A, C and F are more likely to be impacted while areas B, D and E are not.

Systems thinking reveals a variety of patterns – known as systems archetypes (Senge, 1990)[23]. There are several such patterns common in organizations and we provide a catalogue of these in our Expedition Back Pack at the end of this book. One common one is known as "fixes that fail". Here is a description of this pattern:

> A problem cries out for resolution. A solution is implemented that quickly fixes the symptoms of the problem but does not tackle the underlying causes of the problem. The unintended consequences of the "quick fix" are that the problem remains unresolved and manifests itself in other ways later. When the symptoms reappear after a time delay they generally do so at the same or (usually) worse level. The problem is now worse than when we started...

Some organizations repeat fixes that fail and become permanently failing organizations – there are school boards, companies and other organizations that fit into this category (indeed, there is a body of literature dedicated to them[24]). Such organizations represent the consequence of not understanding a pattern.

Identifying Trends and Patterns

Must Look At's

There are some things all organizations have to look systematically at in terms of trends and patterns. These include:

- **Demography** – what impact will changing demographics both locally, regionally, nationally and globally have on the organization? Will it become more or less difficult to recruit and retain staff and leadership personnel? Will the client or customer base of the organization change – what has changed over time and how will these changes continue into the future?

- **Finances** – what can we see as trends and patterns with respect to the flow of money in and out of the organization? When we draw trend lines for costs versus revenue what do we see?

- **Technology** – will current and emerging technologies have an impact on the work of the organization or system under review? Can technology change how the organization/system offers its services or conducts its work? What are the positive and negative trends with respect to technology which the organization needs to account for?

- **Competition** – No matter what the service or product or organization is, someone is seeking to offer an alternative to that product or service. Whether it is health care, education or other established public services new approaches and models of delivery are emerging all the time. What can be seen on the competitive landscape which could change the way in which the organization operates? For example, in education the growth of private tutoring, the emergence of online learning options (e.g. The Khan Academy) and new approaches to the support of special needs learners can all be seen to suggest trends which any foresight exercise should take into account. In our recent work on post-secondary education[25] we were surprised at how many such trends were impacting post-secondary education in the developed world.

In exploring these four areas, other areas emerge. For example, in education the question of governance and accountability would emerge from a discussion of several of these topics as a clear domain in which new trends and patterns can be seen.

Might Look At's

As you explore the above areas of trends and patterns, others will emerge. Michael Porter[26] suggests that there are five forces working on an organization which have an impact on its future. These five forces are:

1. **Threat of New Entrants** – what is the possibility that some new organization could enter the market or provide the service you provide and reduce your customer / client base and change the "game"? For example, when the *iPhone* offered photography and the ability to capture images quickly and simply, what happened to *Kodak*?

2. **The Threat of Substitution of Products or Services You Provide** – An existing player in the sector you operate in or a new player could offer a substitute to the service you provide and, by doing so, change the basis of your organization. For example, when *Comfree* began to support private house sales for a guaranteed fee, what changes did this lead to in the real estate industry? What impact has Kindle and other e-book readers had on the book industry?

3. **Buying Power of Customers** – when customer behaviour changes then there are clear impacts on an industry and the organizations within it. For example, *Nokia* and *Blackberry* were once dominant players in the business phone sector of the mobile telephone market. *Nokia* has recently sold part of its Smartphone business to *Microsoft* and *Blackberry* is for sale. The reason: customers have chosen the *Apple* and *Samsung* products in preference to these "standard" issue mobile phones. Customers are shaping the market.

4. **Buying Power of Suppliers** – Suppliers can change a sector. For example, when Pearson Corporation began to shift its focus from simply publishing (they are the largest publisher in the world) to a focus on learning systems, then they can change the way in which school boards, colleges and universities think about learning materials. The Government of British Columbia's decision to offer digital textbooks to college and university students in preference to hard-copy textbooks came about due to pressure from suppliers.

5. **Intensity of Rivalry and Competition** – Public and private sector competes and just as private companies compete with each other, so public organizations compete with one other. For example, Catholic

and Public school Boards in major cities in Canada compete for students – they use advertising (television, radio, print), word-of-mouth and other means to attract students. All are publicly funded. This rivalry sometimes turns to collaboration (e.g. in the development of electric cars, competing car manufacturers collaborated on the battery technology), but competition has consequences.

When you look at Porter's five forces, do they suggest trends or patterns that you should consider?

Megatrends are also documented in a variety of places. They include trends such as:

- **The Internet of Things** – where all objects (surfaces, watches, televisions, cars, ovens, etc.) are connected via the internet to each other and can be "managed" from anywhere. Cars send messages to your Smartphone suggesting the need for service; your refrigerator indicates that you are running low on milk and so on. How will growing connectivity of things offer opportunities, challenges or dangers for your organization?

- **Work-Life Balance** – with connectivity being anytime, anywhere balancing work, family, play and leisure is a challenge which also has health and social implications. Is there a trend or pattern here which impacts your organization?

- **Multigenerational Workplace** – At one organization in which I worked there were employees aged between 18 and 75 (no compulsory retirement age). Multiple generations with different expectations about work-life balance, commitment, financial security and different assumptions about the meaning of work and career. What are the implications of this for organizations?

- **Globalization** – it is possible to sit in a remote northern community in Canada and work on securing a degree from a University in Australia. I can order goods from China via e-bay and expect them to arrive within 7-10 days. I can have custom knit clothing created for me in Scotland and delivered to my door in Edmonton. Custom built motorcycles are being designed and built in northern Alberta and shipped around the world. What are the implications of globalization for your organization?

- **3D Printing** – Just as the internet has changed communications and had a major impact on a range of businesses, 3D printing promises a similar impact on the world. Objects that had to be ordered and waited upon – spare parts for a vacuum cleaner or car, new frames for spectacles – can all be printed on a moderately priced device anywhere which has power and internet connectivity. 3D printers are now commercially available. What impact could they have on your organization?

You can look at catalogues of such trends for inspiration – the World Future Society's magazine *The Futurist* documents many such trends and developments each month – and identify those which seem to be relevant and impactful in terms of the future of your organization.

Scouting Parties and Inspired Conversations – A Way of Finding Trends

In our own work, The Innovation Expedition makes a great deal of use of what we term scouting parties. These are systematic approaches to knowledge individuals, teams or organizations that embody or understand the trends and patterns we are exploring. We approach the work of creating a scouting party in a systematic way. Here's how:

We create:

- a list of the top dozen most reputable people in the world working on the problem under consideration and a list of the most reputable research institutions containing skills and expertise related to the challenge being addressed and we approach them for contact time (in person, video conference, audio conference).

We seek to understand:

- the experience of individuals and institutions that have most effectively addressed the problem or issues we are addressing – what have they understood, done, found and experienced?

We develop:

- short case studies of "good practice" presented in such a way as to be useful to other practitioners.
- an analysis of existing viewpoints on the problem or issue, along with their similarities and differences.
- an analysis of what has been tried and found *not* to work.
- an analysis of paths or strategies that have been successful or are

felt to be promising for the future.

Usually two or three people are engaged in each scouting party so as to ensure that the outfitters and champions of the expedition are meaningfully engaged and are actively listening to the experience of others. All of the sightings discovered by the scouting party (we develop...) are documented.

From time to time we also host "inspired conversations". This is where we invite a well known authority to spend time with the strategic foresight team and to present some of their understanding relevant to the topic at hand and then engage in a meaningful dialogue and exploration with those invited. For example, we asked Charles Handy to engage in a conversation with 25 people as part of some strategic foresight work for Heinz or Margaret Wheatley for the Alberta Teachers' Association engaged with over 200 people in a similar way.

Backcasting

Backcasting is another way of unearthing trends. Imagine it is 2050 and you are asked to describe the school system in Alberta. You need to be thorough, not superficial. What does teaching and learning look like? Where does most effective learning occur? What supports and place do those with special needs have? How are First Nations, Inuit and Métis doing and what is different about their education in 2050 from the education system in 2013?

Having understood what is happening in 2050, now take us back each five years from 2050 and back to the present. What happened when? When did individual learning become more dominant than classroom based work? When did the teaching profession change significantly and what were the precursors? Show a timeline 2015 2018, 2023, 2028, 2033, 2038, 2043 and 2050 and describe what happens in each of these time windows – always working back from the future.

This work can be very powerful in helping unearth trends and patterns that then require more detailed evidence gathering to ensure that they are not simply passing fads or temporary "glitches".

Delphi Process

Many find the title of this process mysterious, but in fact it is a very straightforward process. It is a structured technique for eliciting foresight from a panel of experts. A questionnaire is devised which asks a panel (usually between 25 and 100) experts to confidentially and anonymously respond to forecasts about the future. They comment, add and delete forecasts and the questionnaire is then revised and sent back to the panel for further comment. The idea is that the range of forecasts ("answers") will decline as the process continues, with more and more of the panel aligning around the most likely forecasts with detailed reactions to those relegated to "maybe" or "most unlikely" status available for later review. The process continues – maybe 3-4 rounds of surveys to the same panel – until an agreed "stop" point is reached – e.g. achievement of consensus, stability of results, and sufficient number of rounds.

There are several advantages to this method, especially now that the process can be undertaken online using dedicated tools (e.g. *Hyperdelphi*). These include:

- A large number of people can be contacted and engaged in this process since it is asynchronous and can be undertaken anytime and anywhere – in one classic example some 1,454 experts looked at the eLAC Action Plans for Latin America which is widely seen as the most extensive engagement in intergovernmental policy-making in the developing world[27];
- Different panels representing different expertise can be engaged in the same process at the same time – scientists, business leaders, policy makers, consumers and so on.
- Nothing is lost – even "discarded" foresight can prove valuable later.

The use of Delphi has produced a range of results from good to poor, with the poor results often attributed not to the method itself but to the way it was used in particular circumstances. The key requirement for success rests with the selection of the panel itself. If the panelists have only marginal interest or limited knowledge about the topic, especially a technical topic, then the results will be weaker than if the panel were the leading experts in that topic.

One other weakness is that Delphi seeks to secure focus and alignment through consensus building – it is not likely that wild cards and Black Swans will survive this process.

The outcome of a Delphi process is opinion – expert opinion if the panel has been chosen wisely. As such, it is vulnerable to the exact issues we raised in

Chapter 1 about prediction. But there are other issues: (a) low level of expertise at a level of shared expertise across all panelists – some panelists know more than others; (b) results are a function of the way in which the questionnaire used for the Delphi process is worded – ambiguity and uncertainty about intent can skew results; and (c) unless built into the design, the results are generally not weighted by degree of risk and uncertainty.

The Delphi method is best used to explore a single, focused question – there is less evidence of its utility in looking at a range of nested and complex issues – what are sometimes referred to as "swampy problems".

Uncertainty Analysis – Understanding Risk and Uncertainty

Trends and patterns are the cornerstone of strategic foresight, but each trend or pattern involves a degree of uncertainty. For each trend or pattern we need to establish a degree of risk and uncertainty.

The Innovation Expedition uses four levels of uncertainty for each of the trends it identifies in a trend / pattern exploration. These are:

1. **Low Uncertainty** – We have a clear view of the future and our understanding of outcomes and patterns are dependable. We can place a strong bet that we are right.
2. **Moderate Uncertainty** - Limited set of possible outcomes (say two or three), one of which will definitely occur.
3. **Significant Uncertainty** – There are a wide range of possible outcomes, any one of which could occur.
4. **Wild Uncertainty** – There is such an array of outcomes that it is impossible to be sure of any one or any combination occurring. (This is most likely to be a wild card – see below).

If all of our trends have low uncertainty then we have likely missed some developments which will "change the game" – just as many missed the opportunity of being engaged in the personal computing revolution in the 1970s and 1980s (Ken Olson, then Chairman of Digital Equipment Corporation said in 1977, "there is no reason anyone would want a computer in their home"! and IBM rejected the whole idea of the Windows operating system or NOKIA thought of itself as unassailable as the leader in hand-held wireless telephony). Equally, if all of our trends have significant uncertainty or wild uncertainty we are likely not being thorough in our understanding of what the dynamics of the challenge we are addressing really are.

Normally, we will have trends which are predominantly in categories 1 and 2 with a few in 3 and usually no more than one in 4. Remember the motto of scenario planning: *"it's better to be vaguely right than exactly wrong!"*

There are quantitative methods than can be used to explore risk and uncertainty in a more comprehensive way. What we are seeking to do by exploring uncertainty and risk is to map plausible uncertainties – we do not need to evaluate every possible outcome and understanding. This helps us identify the trends and patterns we want to keep "in view" so as to help move to scenario development.

Causal Layer Analysis (CLA)

A growing tool in the armoury of analysts is causal layer analysis – a process by which trends and patterns are discerned from seeking to thoroughly understand the cause of something – the layers of causation. This methodology was developed by Sohail Inayatullah who is a leading futurist and Visiting Professor at the Graduate Institute of Futures Studies at Tamkang University in Taipei, Taiwan.

This technique involves understanding an issue in terms of four "layers":

1. *Litany*: Surface, easily-verified comments such as, "Water shortages are likely." These generally leave speaker and hearer feeling that "someone" should do something. Another example would be "our schools are broken – we should do something to improve them!"

2. *Social Causes*: Statements invoking actors and their structural relationships, such as, "If only government would manage water better there would be no shortages." Or, "We should weed out the poor teachers and train teachers better – give rewards for good student outcomes". These statements tend to suggest incremental policy changes as the solution to problems.

3. *Discourse/Worldview*: Grand, "big picture" statements that challenge assumptions on the previous two levels, such as, "We need a Left-Green water system, not a market system!" Or, "We need to get out of an industrial model of schooling and do much more to personalize learning so as to unleash the creativity of students". The key at this

61

level is to search for positions that reflect deeper, generally non-negotiable worldviews.

4. *Myth and Metaphor:* Folk sayings, slogans, archetypes and ancient stories, such as, "God gave earth to man to do with as he wishes," or a story of water and progress, of man's ingenuity solving the challenges that nature gives us. In our school example, "the best teachers work with students in ways that unleashes talents they didn't know they had – let me tell you about…"

A CLA conducts both a *vertical* analysis, which cuts across layers, and a set of *horizontal* analyses that examine each layer.

This is the analysis work we need to do. But here is how we use this kind of approach in practice:

1. *Undertaking a Vertical Gaze: Uncovering Causality*

   This step exposes the underlying causality of the issue in question. Usually this starts at the Litany level, and then moves through to Myth and Metaphor. At each level, the facilitator may ask prompting questions to guide discussions. For example:

   - Litany: What might a current newspaper headline about this issue look like? Think about the most dramatic headline about the issue…what might it be?
   - Social Causes: How and why did the issue arise? Who is involved? What is the source of the litany? Why was it presented? Who is being quoted – what is their involvement? What are the underlying causes?
   - Discourse/Worldview: Who are the stakeholders? What values do they have? Who usually talks and lobbies about this issue? What do they stand to lose or gain? Who has the most control over the issue?
     Note: As participants become more comfortable with CLA, it is helpful to refer to ideologies, as a way to frame stakeholder views.
   - Myth and Metaphor: What is an image or phrase that encapsulates what has been uncovered so far? What work of fiction, movie, poetry, art, etc. evokes an image of the issue

62

being discussed? Are there any myths that may constrain thinking or acting in relation to this issue? Can you think of a film that really portrays this issue or a story or a drama?

2. *Horizontal Gazes: Discovering Alternatives*
This step asks questions that allow other ways of knowing to be discovered, within a given layer. Initially this takes place at the Social Causes and Discourse/Worldview levels:
   - Social Causes: Use a process known as STEEP (explore the Social, Technical, Environmental, Economic and Political angles and discourse) perspectives to reveal a different understanding of an issue.
   - Discourse/Worldview: Ask, what values have been embodied in the current manifestation of this issue? Are there other perspectives or viewpoints? What are they? What is being written in fringe/periphery journals about this issue? How is the influence of these overviews being contained? What would happen if these other views became dominant? How has this type of issue arisen over time?

3. *Re-Envisioning the Myth and Metaphor*
There are two goals at this stage: 1) Uncover the underlying myths and metaphors that constrain current thinking; and 2) Capturing a new story or image of the collective beliefs that reflect the utopian wishes of the group in regard to the issue. The two visions should then be contrasted.

4. *Recasting the Issue and Defining Possible Solutions*
Starting with the reformulated story/image from the previous step, go up the layers to recast the issue/problem at each level. The "Causal Layered Analysis Table" in the appendices of reference **[1]** can help organize this stage.

5. *Selecting and Documenting Solutions at Each Level*
Select a manageable number of solutions for further use in the foresight process. Usually, this involves selecting one issue or solution from each layer:
   - Litany: Instrumental solutions and quick-fix approaches
   - Social Causes: Policy-oriented solutions
   - Discourse/Worldview: Solutions based on changing the prevailing mindset
   - Myth and Metaphor: Imagery-base solutions

63

Wild Cards

There is a serious rigour associated with trend analysis and pattern recognition, as you will see. But sometimes it is important to include what is known as a "wild card". A wild card is something that may not be a trend or an existing pattern but "could just happen". For example, imagine the Pope deciding to permit the ordination of women or to abandon the celibacy rule for Catholic priests. These are highly unlikely possibilities – indeed, all who understand the authority of the Papacy and have studied the history of the Catholic church would say that they are highly unlikely. But what if the Pope did one of these things – how would it change the Catholic Church and its place in society?

What if a Minister of Education decided to convert all public schools currently run by School Boards (or Local Education Authorities in the UK) to be privately managed? Sounds farfetched? Yet this is the exact wild card being used by the Secretary of State for Education in England – Rt. Hon. Michael Gove, MP. By January 2013, some 2,600 English schools (12% of all schools and over 50% of all English High Schools) had opted out of the control of Local Education Authorities and are free to set their own admission standards, recruit teachers to teach (including teachers without a teaching qualification), set teacher pay levels and receive the same funds as a publicly managed school would receive. There are 28 local authorities where at least 1 in 5 schools is now an open academy, as these schools are called. In almost all of the 129 local authorities, at least 1 in 5 secondary schools is an open academy. There are 10 local authorities where at least 1 in 5 primary schools is now an open primary academy. Schools are converting all the time – by May of 2013, an additional 150 schools had converted since the start of 2013. The intent is for all schools in England to be managed in this way. While at this time, the academies and free schools are all non-profit "social enterprises", Michael Gove has made clear that he intends to permit these to convert to for-profit enterprises if a Conservative government wins a majority in the 2015 election. No longer a wild card, this is now public policy.

Here is another wild card. What if the earth entered a cooling trend? We know that the various analysis of climate using computer models all suggest the opposite, but there is evidence that the earth is cooling. For example, there has been no significant change in the global mean surface temperature for 18 years, the Arctic ice extent in 2013 is the largest it has ever been and solar activity is at a record low over the last 100 years. Some scientists, by no means all, are suggesting that we could be returning to a Little Ice age (1450-1850), which could be 4°C cooler than at present. What would be the impact on our communities if this was the case?

Or another: what if a technological breakthrough allowed the long-term storage of energy at a very low cost? For example, being able to store wind or solar energy at a very low cost would transform the energy systems of many countries.

Or another: what if developments in stem cell research enabled health systems to restore damaged organs, including the pancreas, by efficient implants of stem cells which had been "trained" to grow the replacement organ for damaged ones?

These are all low probability events in the period to 2050 (but all of them except the first are possible), but you now understand the idea of the wild card. In our work on scenario planning, there is a need to look at these wild cards (brainstorming, searching for outliers in the science, policy and engineering communities, literature review of the skeptical literature) and ask: is there one or two wild cards which would be "game changing" that we should consider?

Having Found a Trend or Pattern, What Now?

Once having identified a trend or pattern, you think it is important to consider you first need to define exactly what the trend is and what evidence there is that this trend can have a serious impact on your organization. For example, if you determine that demography is important to consider as part of your strategic foresight expedition, exactly what is it about demography do you need to consider and exactly what impact do you think this trend could have on your organization? Look at the table below and consider how you might complete it for the trends you identify. We have used it to look at some trends a school district identified during their review of demographic trends.

Trend / Pattern	Evidence	Impact
Increasing Student Numbers	6% annual growth in students seeking admission to the school district yet only a 1% growth in	• Overcrowding of schools to cope with demand • Large class size • Teacher stress • Breeching of

	capacity	collective agreements
Shorter Career Span of Teachers	Teachers staying in the district on average of 8.5 years (down from 11 3 years, years ago)	• Cultural shifts in schools continuously • Difficulty securing stable staffing models • Leaders recruited with less teaching experience than ever before (down from an average of 14 years in 2000 to 6 years in 2013)
Days Lost to Illness and Stress of Teachers	Teacher stress and illness now accounts for 4% of available teaching hours in the district – up from 2.4% in 2000	• Growing demand for teacher substitutes – getting more difficult to find • Difficulty securing stable staffing models • Critical reason for shorter career span for teachers in the District

Evidence Review

Evidence is the key to this table. When we look at trends, we need to establish how "real" they are. For example, if we were to look at 3D Printing and schools or health care, we could indicate that they are currently present only in a small number of very specific cases for very specific reasons. However, when we look at requests for new technology in health care, we can see demand rising. If we investigate why the demand is rising, we can see that many surgeons can see convenience and potential cost-reduction in custom manufacture of specific items used in surgery on-site. This may be worth looking at – we don't know until we dig into the evidence.

We do this work for each of the trends we identify – we may have 30-40 in our catalogue and this requires a fair bit of work. For example, in a foresight exercise related to the bioeconomy of a jurisdiction, we identified 15 trends which would impact the future of the sector. Each deserves investigation, unless the early review of evidence suggests that there is no trend or pattern or that, even though there is, the potential impact on the organization is so small as to be not worth considering. For example, it may be far too early to look at the impact of 3D printing in a school system.

Prioritization

Once the evidence review is completed, there is often a need to cull the trend/pattern list to a manageable number. The first task is to "lump" like trends together. For example, two items in our table above – shorter career span of teachers and days lost to illness and stress – can be combined into Changing Patterns of Teaching Careers.

Having done as much "lumping" as we can to reduce overlap and duplication, we now need to prioritize. The question we are asking is: which of the trends will have most impact in the time-span we are considering? If we are looking at 2050, then 3D Printing may be "in", for example, but if we are looking at 2020 it may not be.

There are a variety of ways to prioritize a list of trends. Ranking against a weighted range of criteria (scale of impact on the system as a whole, cost of the impact, impact of the trend on people in the organization) for example. But the first question to ask before we talk about "*how* to prioritize" is "*who* should prioritize?"

When we get to the point at which the trends are understood and have been culled, it is critical to involve the champions, the outfitters and key influencers. This is a critical task in the expedition and there is a need for strong ownership of the decisions made. Including or excluding a trend could greatly influence all subsequent aspects of the expedition. To make the point: what if the International Panel on Climate Change (IPCC) had agreed at the outset that not only CO_2 was a factor in climate change but so was the sun and the ocean systems, we would now be engaged in a very different conversation about how to respond to the changing climate[28]. Choosing the trends to focus on will determine the journey the strategic foresight expedition will take. It is therefore crucial that all who have been engaged and who have strategic influence should make these choices.

Card Sorts

One way which has been found very useful in terms of prioritizing trends is to use what is known as a card-sort technique. Each trend is placed on an item card – one trend per card. Participants are asked then to sort these cards into categories – from Most Critical to Least Critical (we usually have five categories – Most Critical, Critical, Somewhat Important, Least Critical, and Not Sure). We ask small groups of 3-5 to do this and have several groups do this.

What we find is that some trends appear in the top two categories across all groups. Other trends are in different places in different groups. An activity aimed at exploring which trends should be in which category - discussion and analysis – can be very insightful in terms of creating a priority list of trends.

There are now software systems which enable this to be done online at a low cost. In our own organization we are using *usabiliTEST* as the software of choice. This enables users around the world to sort cards into categories and the software provides a variety of analysis tools.

Connecting Trends

We mentioned in Chapter 2 that there was a morphological process associated with trend analysis that needs to be considered. Let us look at what this looks like.

We first construct a chart showing the trends, patterns and wild cards we have prioritized. The chart may look something like the one below, where our "understanding" of a Trend is captured in each of the "understanding" boxes. For example, our understanding that part of the demography trend is demand for student placement exceeds supply, class size grows, and teacher turnover grows and so on:

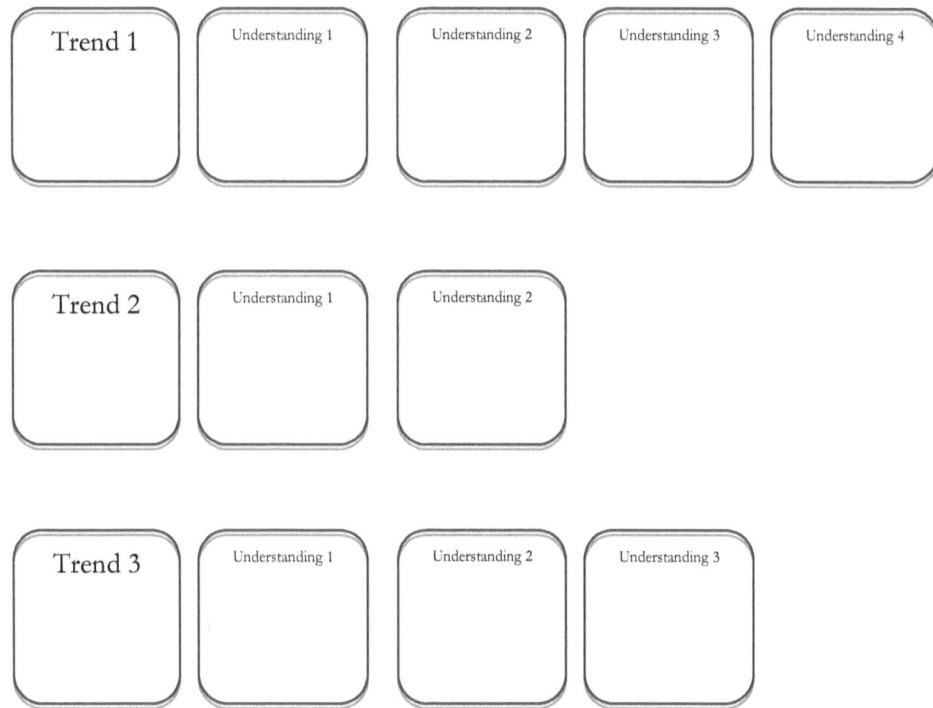

Figure 2: Mapping Trends in a Simple Box Diagram

What happens next is simple. We look for linkages between the understandings by drawing arrows to reflect the connections we see. This could look something like the figure below:

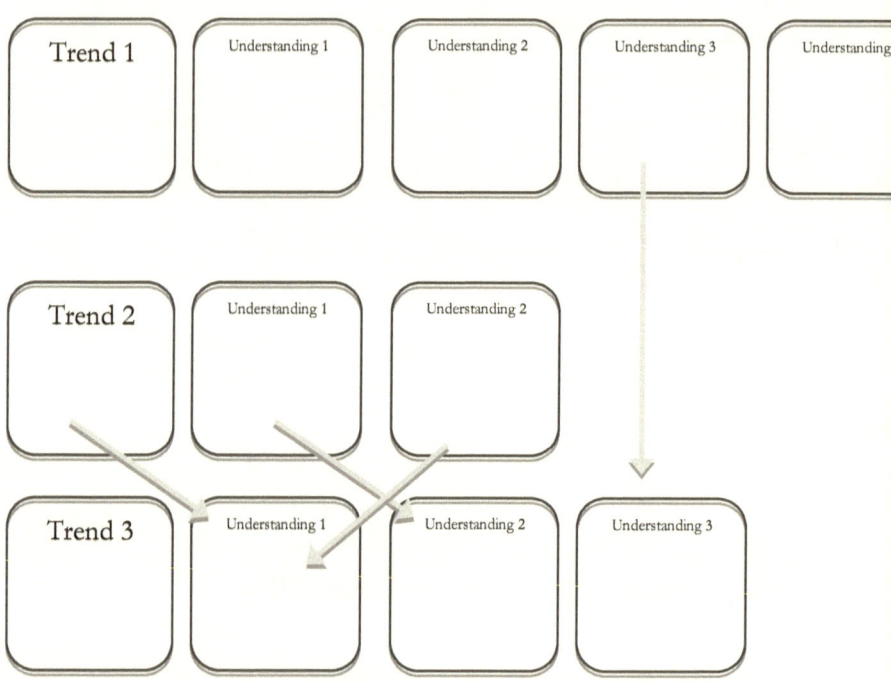

Figure 3: Connections Between Understanding – Starting Point for Scenarios

What is being done here is looking for the linkages so that we can build a map of connections – a morphological understanding – of how the trends and patterns are interacting so that we can see the shape of things to come. You will find this mapping activity very helpful in building scenarios. Indeed, we use large Post-it notes for the understandings so as to be able to move them into columns, with each column reflecting components of a potential scenario.

Some Dangers

There are some dangers associated with trend-spotting and pattern-recognition and we need to be mindful of these as we undertake this phase of the expedition. Three in particular are important to bear in mind.

First, there is the danger of selecting trends that suit our strategic intent rather than looking at all trends, no matter whether they will have a positive or negative impact on where we hope our organization or sector will go. For example, if you begin by rejecting any trend which does not fit your pre-determined outcome, you will end up being overly selective in what you look at.

Second, there is the danger of over-estimating the impact of a trend. Many will remember the genuine concerns raised about the implications of moving from 1999 to 2000 from a time control on devices point of view – the Millennium Bug. Many thought that a vast range if equipment from aircraft to ships, trains and automobiles as well as banking systems and other technologies would simply stop working as the clock mechanisms built into computers were only programmed for 1900 dates. Several billion dollars were spent on teams trying to ensure that this would not be a serious "disaster". It wasn't. Our estimate of impact was over-blown. Imagine this same danger for the trends you think are most critical.

Finally, there is the danger of elevating a wild card into a major trend. You have met people who are very passionate about an idea or a principle and will not let it go. The idea, for example, that the ocean levels are rising so fast that large parts of New York will be under water. Anyone doing the math on current data sets will know that this is possible some 27,000 years from now – but some individuals are convinced that this could happen "anytime soon". Or economists who are convinced that governments should not be funding R&D since it "distorts markets". Or, well we could go on. A wild card is a remote possibility that could happen in the time span you are concerned with (say by 2025, 2050 or 2075) but there are no guarantees. Don't let the wild card become the main card.

Conclusion

Many find this work very rewarding. It is essentially evidence-based analysis of the driving forces which will change and impact the organization or industry you are looking systematically at. What is rewarding is that you begin to fully understand and connect trends which most of the time we are only vaguely aware of.

Trend and pattern analysis is a core component of strategic foresight. It permits the systematic development of understanding futures. But it is not the end. The next task – using these trends to build scenarios – is the key task in connecting these trends and beginning to map different futures.

Chapter 6: Scenarios of the Future – The Process of Scenario Planning

In January 2007 Steve Ballmer, then CEO of Microsoft, said, "There's no chance that the iPhone is going to get any significant market share. No chance."

Introduction

The key method widely used in strategic foresight work is scenario planning. We devote this chapter to an examination of what it is, how it used and what its limitations are.

How Do We Develop Scenarios?

When we look at the future, four possible domains of the future can be discerned. We show these in the figure below.

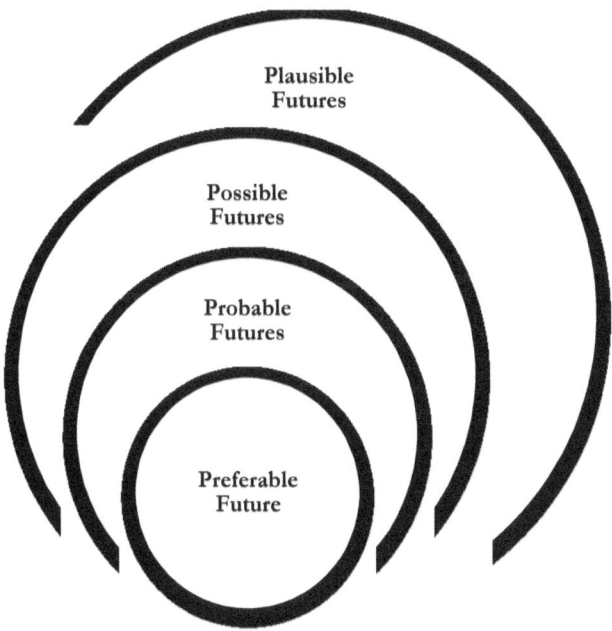

Figure 4: Domains of the Future

The key purpose of scenario planning is to discern which patterns/trends fall into which of these domains. The aim is not to begin and end with the identification of the preferred future, but to represent several different versions of the future in a systematic and thorough way. Doing this work proactively – rehearsing for multiple futures – builds organization resilience and capacity to respond to change.

Scenario planning is a thorough, evidence-based process – it is not speculation or guesswork. It is based on the strategic foresight expedition model outlined in Chapter 2 and requires extensive review and analysis of information and data from a variety of sources, as we saw in the previous chapter.

The benefit of this work is that it builds organizational capacity. In particular:

- It enables organizations to review their assumptions about both their past and their present state – a process that often produces insights and new understanding.
- It helps organizations identify new opportunities for growth and development before they become mainstream.
- It focuses the organization on risks and uncertainties and helps the organization develop more robust approaches which mitigates risk and helps to leverage opportunities.
- Creates a more learning oriented and adaptive organization – one which begins to manage and leverage knowledge more directly.
- It creates strategically aligned and focused teams within and across the organization.

If this is what we are seeking to achieve, how do we do it? Let us look at each of the components of the work of scenario development. We have developed a six-step approach to this work, though others have different versions for this process.

Step 1: Understanding Trends, Patterns and Wild Cards

The work of scenario planning begins with the development of rich, evidence-based stories about the future. Take a simple question: if we do nothing differently from our current practices, what will happen to our school system in Alberta by 2050? We then explore the answer to this question from a variety of perspectives – e.g. from a community perspective, a student perspective, teacher perspective, Principal and so on. We gather evidence of the narratives at play in each of these domains and explore the assumptions behind these narratives as well as the evidence that supports them.

We can use interviews, literature reviews, meta-analysis and other forms of scanning. We can use scouting parties to speak to leading educators, those engaged in planning the school system, backcasting and so on. The task is to build a catalogue of trends, patterns and wild cards, assess the risk and uncertainty for each and then prioritize, just as we outlined in the previous chapter.

At this stage the task is to scan to understand.

Step 2: Emerging Issues Analysis
The narratives and stories we explored in Step 1 suggest a catalogue of issues that we need to fully understand. We need to move past a collection of "stories" and into a systematic catalogue of key themes and issues which all of our scenarios need to address. This is sometimes referred to as morphological analysis.

Take one theme – demography and its impact on the school system - as an example. When we review the narratives we may see some answers to the question, "What impact will changing demography have on the school system in Alberta?" There are unlikely to be a large number of different responses to this question – usually we find 3-5 such responses.

If we then look at the question, "What impact will the financing of schools have on Alberta's school system if the current regime does not change?" We may also have 5-6answers. If we explore the catalogue of answers, we can soon begin to build a picture of "most likely responses" for each category we explore together with a short list of "wild cards" that we need to take into account.

One hundred stories may now become a total of 25 answers to 7 questions. We can then start to identify patterns in these responses – a first step to building multiple scenarios.

Step 3: Understanding the Dominant Themes – The Uncertainties that Will Shape the Future
For our topic there may be key trends and patterns that we also need to identify. Staying with our Alberta schools example, we may have identified nine key trends and patterns and one wild card that really will shape the future of the Alberta school system. We need then to interrogate these trends and patterns and locate two or three dominant themes. These may well be topics

such as: (a) continued expansion of demand with inadequate funding; (b) individualized learning; and (c) changing nature of instruction and the teaching profession. These three "big themes" become dominant – umbrella themes which capture several trends and patterns.

What we are essentially looking at when we describe dominant themes are areas of uncertainty. For example, the collective learning versus individualized learning may be seen as a dimension of uncertainty – sometimes we need to be at one end of this spectrum and at other times there is a need to be at the other.

Step 4: Synthesize Analysis in Steps 1-3 Into A Set of Scenarios
Now we have a lot of information. We have evidence-based trends, patterns and stories that help us understand the future. We have three or four dominant themes. We need to find a simple way of connecting disparate themes and ideas into a coherent set of scenarios.

There are different methods in use here, but the most common is to look for two key dimensions that define the space in which we can see the future fitting. For example, one dimension we could look at in our forest example might be *demands for growth – constrained budgets* and another *individualized learning versus conventional education*. Using these two dimensions (one vertical one horizontal) together might then suggest four scenarios as a starting point for our conversation. We could illustrate this with the diagram below.

Demand for Growth

Individualized Learning

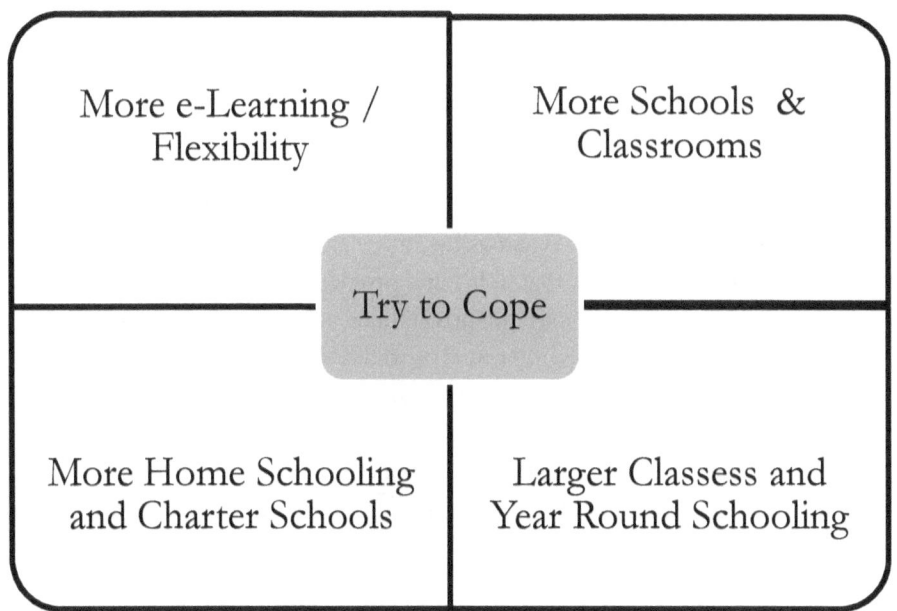

More e-Learning / Flexibility	More Schools & Classrooms
Try to Cope	
More Home Schooling and Charter Schools	Larger Classess and Year Round Schooling

Constrained Budgets

Figure 5: Scenario Matrix

We are interested in more than one scenario and often develop some 16 to 20 at an early stage of this synthesis work. By then classifying them into our preferred, probable, possible and plausible categories we begin to "cull" the number down from (in one case, 50) a large number to a group of manageable scenarios we can more fully understand.

Let us look at a concrete example in more detail. *Wired* magazine explored the question: "What will the nature of commerce be like in 2020?" (They did this in 2010). Following a brainstorming of trends and some backcasting (see previous Chapter); they identified two critical dimensions, which they refer to as uncertainties.

The first axis of uncertainty is the character of our desire, an "I" or "We," individual or community. This uncertainty about the quality of our individual hopes and intentions cuts at the most fundamental level: Will the energy of democratization and the ascendance of the ultimate individualized "I" continue to prevail? Or, will our social organization and self-definition be rooted in a group – *a* nation, a tribe, a collection of users of a particular brand, a more communitarian "We"? The *I* or the *We* will never disappear, but which will come to be the prevailing influence in our culture? It could go either way, and with a bang; that is the uncertainty.

The second (vertical) axis shows the uncertain character of social structure: Will society be a center that holds and provides stability, or will it fragment? Here, we stake out the extreme possibilities of social organization: Will social and political structures (either new or traditional) provide a society wide coherence and order? Or, will society shatter into shards, the jagged edges of which do not mesh into a coherent whole? Will there be a state to impose order, level the playing field, and unify a commonwealth? Or, will permanent fragmentation, increasing plurality, and unfettered free-markets bring us to "bottom-up" functioning anarchy?

The second uncertainty might seem at first blush an outcome of the first. But in fact, while they are related, they are separately uncertain. Indeed, it is precisely the way they are intertwined that makes them interesting by giving us four scenarios, four very different "future spaces" to explore. We can see these four spaces in this scenario model below:

Fragmentation

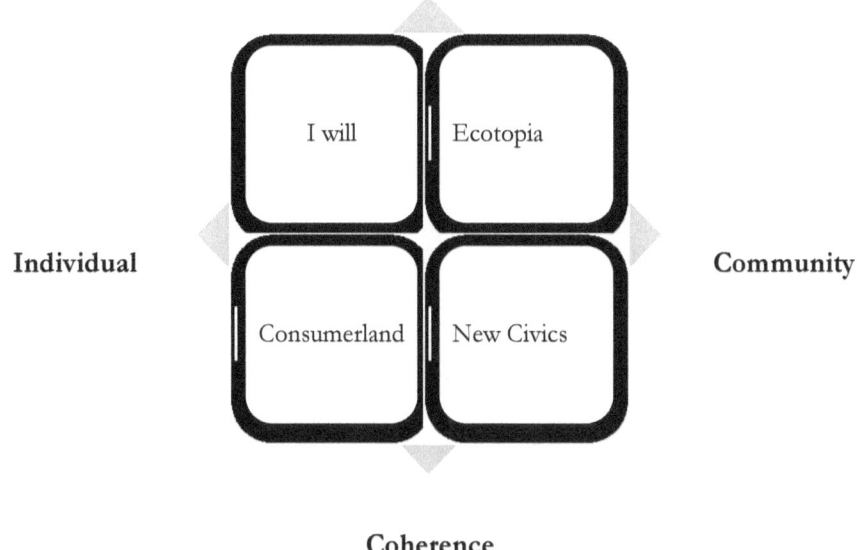

Individual

I will

Ecotopia

Consumerland

New Civics

Community

Coherence

Figure 6: Future Scenarios for Commerce in 2020

Here's how the *Wired* scenarios play out in each of the four corners:

1. **I Will** is the quadrant where individualism (I-ness) meets fragmentary or marginal control by large organizations. It is a future in which you want and get the ability to make your life uniquely yours. The internet is the ubiquitous medium through which you realize your desires and discharge your few and relatively unimportant social duties. Government has withered in the face of privatization, replaced by a largely electronic marketplace that connects and clears transactions of every type. Most large, centralized institutions have crumbled into a much more finely grained pattern, a many-to-many landscape on which each individual is alternately producer and user. In this future, you co-produce the products and experiences that you consume. Your loyalty is to your tools, knowledge, and skills.

2. **Consumerland** is the quadrant where individual desires meet a social and corporate center. It is a future in which everyone is the ultimate consumer, possessed of almost infinite choices. The Net is again a ubiquitous medium – *but* a medium through which corporations deliver marketing messages tailored directly to your unique preferences, via personal catalogs, personalized ads and coupons, and the like. The products, of course, are "mass customized" to your desires. Government plays an active role, laying down the rules (standards, regulations) by which corporations play. Social organizations proliferate but it is clear that they serve individual yearnings. The citizen becomes a consumer - served by society.

3. **Ecotopia** is the quadrant where a communal sense of "We" meets a strong social center. It is the future where the center holds. Government plays a large role in supporting the commonwealth, but more important than government is the emergence of widely shared ecological values. These are not coercive values but a voluntary embrace of cohesion, cooperation, and reduced consumption, backed by legislation and even corporate policies. The Net acts as replacement technology; it is maximized to eliminate the need to travel on business, to cut down on the amount of paper used, etc.

4. **New Civics** is a future in which values are shared but in many small, competing groups. It is a decentralized world of tribes, clans, "families," networks, and gangs. It is a future in which we want to build and enjoy the benefits of community but without the help of a benevolent Big Brother government. The Net encourages each group to move most of its members' economic activity and their social services inside a closed group. Thus, government's role and influence are eclipsed by the sway of these emergent groups; small – *often* deadly – *conflicts* among groups pop up continually around the globe. Our primary concern is to be good members of our group. Our loyalty is to its membership, its mores, and its brands. While this future conjures visions of organized crime and sectarian strife, it is also a future of pride, heroism, and the satisfactions of belonging.

These four scenarios provide a way of looking at trends and patterns in a future-focused way – they describe four very different futures. They are "catch-all's" in which we can see the world through very different lenses.

Let us look at a second example so as to make the point about the journey from trends and patterns to scenarios clear.

In 2008, a group convened at the White House to discuss the future of the global economy, given the economic meltdown that was occurring. While others worked on "solving today's problem" through stimulus and government action, others worked on "what's next?" They did so under the instruction of the President of the United States.

They identified two critical uncertainties:

1. **Depth, duration and nature of the downturn in the global economy**. Some depressions and economic shocks – the Great Depression, the oil price shock of 1973, impact of war – can be short (12-18 months) or long (3-12 years). Optimistic views of the 2007-8 crisis suggested it would be over by 2010 and more pessimistic views put the recovery to 2012 or 2015. Underlying this is the issue of whether the situation was cyclical (short-term) or structural economic change (long-term). Was this the end of growth, as some suggested?

2. **The Role of Government versus the Role of the Market in the Recovery**. Keynesian economists suggested that the government should play a pivotal role until unemployment fell to pre-crisis levels, while others took the view that markets were the only way to "return to normal". The key dimension here could be labeled interventionist versus free market.

Using these two dimensions of uncertainty we could construct a simple scenario frame which looks like this:

Intervention

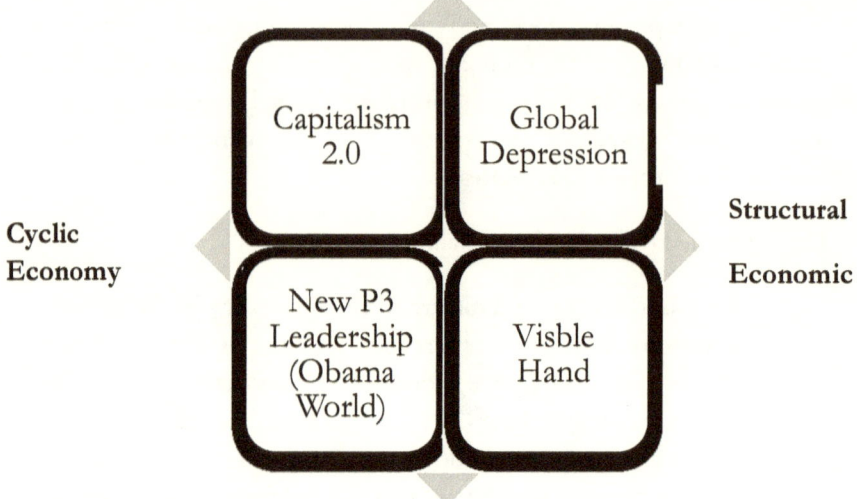

Cyclic Economy

Structural Economic

Market Response

Figure 7: The Future Economy to 2012 (developed in 2008)

In brief, the four scenarios look like this:

1. **Capitalism 2** – Given that this is a conventional recession, the economy should rebound on its own accord with the normal supports provided by Government. Having undertaken stimulus, the Government should step back and let "business as usual" return.

2. **Global Depression** – Governments undertake some stimulus, seek to reduce debt and practice austerity but whatever they do appears too timid to stave off a global double dip recession, mass unemployment and a great depression.

3. **The Visible Hand** – Given that the economy faces structural change, government uses the power of the state to correct, adjust and modify economic drivers (interest rates, quantitative easing, inflation management, subsidies for housing and energy, wage constraints, etc.)

so as to minimize the direct impact of change but also to enable markets to adjust.

4. **New P3 Leadership (Obama World)** – Given that the challenge to the economy is short-term and cyclical, new alliances between government and industry focused on innovation, acceleration of access to new markets, aggressive pursuit of "level playing field" policies through the World Trade Organization and other mechanisms permits recovery to be accelerated but new alliances and partnerships created which could weather another storm.

– you can determine for yourself which path the Obama administration took in its first term and compare and contrast their actions with those, say, of the European Union.

The point of these two cases is to make clear that the detailed and thorough work on trends and patterns led to the development of thinking frameworks for the future. Scenarios are just that – ways of understanding the future that permit analysis.

Step 5: Outline Indicators for Each Scenario
The danger at this stage is to "opt for one" and say that this is the preferred scenario. But remember – our work is to fully understand all of the scenarios we develop.

The key to looking at these scenarios in depth is to identify the indicators that the scenarios we have outlining are occurring. When we described Shell's anticipation of the oil price shock of 1973 we pointed out that they maintained a systematic track of the status of all of the scenarios they developed so that they could anticipate which scenario was emerging when.

For the economic scenario just outlined, the teams worked on indicators for each scenario. For example, here are two sets for the Capitalism 2.0 and Visible Hand – the team, working in 2010, said that these indicators should be clear by 2012:

Capitalism 2.0
- Government withdraws from industry partnerships created to "solve" the crisis

- More international collaboration with respect to banking, stock trade risk and uncertainty – more regulatory authorities in place with strong teeth and tools
- Emerging economies (especially China, India, Brazil) at the table in economic talks and strategy
- Growth in GDP back to normal levels
- Unemployment at pre-crisis levels
- IPOs for Government held banks and companies now frequent – market regains ownership of temporary state assets
- Business Schools revamp their curriculum with a strong emphasis on ethics, accountability, community and corporate social responsibility
- Stock market back to 2007 pre-crisis levels and housing starts growing fast
- Invest in clean energy and innovative technology return to pre-2007 levels

Visible Hand

- Public disapproval of excess – e.g. bonus pay, tax avoidance, CO_2 emissions, large pay-outs for executives who are retiring or "let go"
- Increased protectionism at every level – State, National, International
- Growth remains flat but this is "traded off" against stability and social calm
- Strong and growing sense of community and community engagement
- New social contract between firms and community and new levels of corporate social responsibility
- Stock price of brands associated with luxury goods and the elite fall dramatically
- Church attendance growing
- New interest in government employment and careers in non-profit and social agencies
- Increased regulatory controls in all sectors of the economy
- New high-levels of government investment in health care, education and infrastructure

– the same level of detail was completed for all four scenarios.

The reason the work is done at this level of detail is to deepen the organization's understanding of each scenario and to begin to develop organizational resilience. As they begin to see more of the indicators for one or more scenario they can recognize where these data are headed in terms of pattern and opportunity. You should see this part of the work as "signposts for the future".

One other activity is often done at this stage. Developing stories from within one of these scenario frames set in the future. For example, what is the story we can tell about the Visible Hand from the perspective of a CEO, a Government Minister or a 45-year-old female worker? What does the experience of being in the scenario look and feel like? This often puts flesh on the bare bones statements and indicators we have just developed.

Step 6: Identifying the Preferred Scenario
Scenarios, like the ones we have just outlined:

1. Expand our thinking and understanding not just of the future but of the present.
2. Uncover inevitable or near-inevitable future developments that we can anticipate, many of which are beyond the typical three year planning horizon of most organizations.
3. Build resilience – by identifying signposts to the future we can respond nimbly and quickly to emerging events since we understand both context and complexity of what is emerging.
4. Protect against groupthink – by looking at a range of different futures we don't get stuck in the groupthink which many engage in (look at the Steve Balmer quote at the head of this chapter). Scenarios are vehicles by which individuals and teams can challenge the conventional wisdom and "the future is a straight line from the past" thinking.

But we can't just stop with our framework and details in place; we need to connect the organization to its future. Indeed, one of the dangers which McKinsey Co. identifies with scenario planning[29] is that organizations discard scenarios too quickly. Organizations chose those scenarios which are nearest to their current scenarios and disregard those which challenge the status quo or suggest radical rethinking – like the way in which the Conservative Party's reforms on education in England were dismissed as "unlikely" as recently as 2010 (see description in previous chapter of Wild Cards).

McKinsey[30] suggest some simple rules:

1. Always develop and articulate at least four scenarios.
2. Always describe the signposts and warning signals for each scenario.
3. Always name scenarios with simple, yet memorable ("catchy") names so that they can get used frequently in conversation.
4. Never focus a scenario on a single variable (e.g. growth versus decline) – ensure that the scenarios reflect the complexity of the issues at hand.
5. Classify the developed scenarios into preferred, probable, possible, plausible.

The preferred scenario is the one the organization finds most attractive for its future. The temptation is to just work on this one scenario. This would be a mistake. Given the time-scales we are dealing with, the chances of just one scenario playing out over the entire time under consideration are small. There is a need to look in-depth at *all* of the probable, possible and plausible scenarios, with most emphasis on the preferred and the probable.

So which is the preferred scenario? There are different answers to this question, but the key elements to consider are:

1. Which scenario enables the organization / industry to leverage its existing resources and competencies?
2. Which scenario provides the opportunity for the organization / industry to create and develop competitive or jurisdictional advantage?
3. Which scenario contains the most signposts that are visible now?
4. Which scenario carries the opportunity for the organization/ industry to demonstrate leadership in its sector / community over the longest period of time?

Whichever scenario that holds out the promise of a positive response to all four of these questions should be regarded as the preferred scenario.

A successful scenario planning exercise is not a one-time event. Instead, it is woven into senior management decision-making in several different ways. In part, this integration occurs through osmosis, as the language of the stories is incorporated into senior management conversations. The accuracy of the scenarios is less important than the types of strategic conversations and discussions they spark. This conversation – which of the available scenarios is our preferred future? – is a critical conversation – it is one of the pinnacles of the strategic foresight expedition.

Step 7: Commit to Strategic Action

We now have done a great deal of work – narrowed our "big scan" into some ways of thinking about the future patterns and shapes we will experience: our scenarios. What now?

We need to move from understanding and analysis to a planning and action mode. We have to ask these questions:

- Given the preferred future scenario, what do we need to change in our skills, behaviour and processes to enable that future to be more probable?
- Given the preferred future scenario, who do we need to build partnerships and alliances with to enable that future to be more probable?
- Given the preferred future scenario, what risks do we need to manage and mitigate?
- Given the preferred future scenario, what tracking activities do we need to engage in to monitor whether other probable scenarios are emerging?
- Given the preferred future scenario, what communications and engagement activities do we need to commit to so as to ensure that all in our organization see the future possibilities and opportunities?

In short, we need to align this scenario work with strategic planning and an action plan. Understanding and sharing that understanding does not necessarily lead to action. We will explore these questions in a later chapter.

The Limitations of Scenarios

It is our experience that this is very interesting work – teams and those engaged in this phase of the expedition get very involved and engaged. But we need to be aware of the limitations of what this work represents.

In an important paper tracing the history and documenting the variety of approaches to scenario planning, Meitzner and Reger (2005)[31] indicate that there are these limitations:

- The process of scenario planning is time-consuming, no matter which approach is taken. It is also expensive in terms of person-hours and the seniority of the people who need to be truly engaged for the work to have strategic impact.
- Trend analysis requires a deep and certain knowledge of the field under investigation. "Amateurs" exploring the future of medical technology, for example, have naïve views as to what it takes to secure a change in medical practice and the adoption of new approaches (e.g. regenerative medicine).
- Trend analysis is a technical skill requiring a great deal of access to literature, experts and resources which many organizations are reluctant to provide. The consequence is that many scenario activities are "half baked" and incomplete.
- "Wishful thinking" unduly influences scenario work – the hard core "reality tests" are not performed with sufficient determination.
- Scenario work has been adopted by large corporations and is rarely used by smaller organizations, especially non-profits. There is little documented evidence of the success of this approach in such small organizations.
- There is very little empirical research looking at the impact of scenario work on organizational performance.

We should contrast these limitations with the strengths of the approach, with these, same authors suggest are:

- Scenarios move organizations away from seeking accurate predictions of the future and focus instead on a range of possible futures which the organization needs to be ready to respond to. Doing so aids organization's resilience.
- Scenarios open the organizations leadership to new possibilities and opportunities.
- Scenarios help to identify "weak signals" and potential "wild cards" that need to be tracked and monitored.

- Scenarios greatly aid communication across the organization – especially in terms of being able to articulate the preferred future for the organization.
- Scenarios inform strategic thinking and planning.

In pursuing this work, the outfitter team needs to minimize the limitations and maximize the advantages of the use of scenarios across the organization.

Conclusion

Arie de Geus, who developed the process used by Royal Dutch Shell, has said that

> *"scenarios are stories. They are works of art rather than scientific analysis. The reliability of their content is less important than the types of conversations and decisions that they spark".*

– suggesting that the process of developing scenarios is as important as the use we make of them. He is right. The key to scenario planning is being able to develop a compelling view of the future which spurs action: this is what we are seeking to achieve.

Chapter 7: Using Video, Visualization and Images to Capture the Future

Introduction

On several occasions in the last few chapters, we have mentioned the importance of stories and narrative as ways of bringing scenarios to life. In this short chapter – just a few pages – we want to strengthen this idea by exploring the value of images, visualization and video to bring scenarios to life. This is difficult to do "on paper", but we can make the point with some simple suggestions and links to other resources.

New technology has changed the communication process. Providing visual images to a broader audience has become easy, fast and high quality. Visualization can provide the public and decision-makers a clear idea of the proposed policies, plans and scenarios. Improvement makes information instantly or intuitively understandable. These new technologies have made it possible to communicate what the scenarios may look like when they emerge. These technologies include visualization resources, scenarios as games, simulation and scenario-documentaries.

Story Telling and Narrative as Building Blocks for Understanding

In an earlier text, Albert Mills and I developed an understanding of dynamics within an organization based on structural dynamic systems of communication. The book – *Organizational Rules*[32] - presented an analysis of the ways in which the narratives told within an organization – the implicit and tacit rules – shaped organizational behaviour. Our point was that the informal and formal communications within an organization told the "story" (or more accurately, stories and fantasies) about the organization which shaped the belief and value-system of the organization, which in turn shapes behaviour. The book used models developed in family therapy and systems-thinking to explore how organizations came to function as they do. Such is the power of narrative.

For example, it was said in one organization that the CEO was such an emotional person that any news which wasn't good would throw her into a rage. While this had happened once, it was a unique occurrence but had become "legend" in the organization. Thus, whenever bad news occurred it was disguised or not allowed to be presented to the CEO. The result: the CEO remained out-of-touch and was constantly surprised by the poor performance of some units. She kept firing those who were responsible for these underperforming units who, in turn, were replaced by those who were led to believe the legend (now reinforced by the firings) and so the problems persisted. Things changed when a new Vice President arrived who ignored the legend and he began briefing her on all aspects of the state of the organization – good and bad. The organization substantially improved its performance not because of the new Vice President's exceptional leadership skills, but because he changed the narrative.

To bring scenarios to life, we need to tell stories and show what the scenarios mean to various groups of people. These stories can be presented as:

- Case studies of the organization five, 10 and 15 years from now.
- Individual stories (with photographic montage) written from the future and in the voice of key actors in that future – in a school system it would be students, teachers, Principals, Superintendent and Trustees.
- Photo stories with captions.
- Visualizations of the future in numbers – showing what each of the scenarios would look like in terms of critical indicators but doing so using visualization tools.
- Video stories of the future – such as Corning's "the internet of everything" video which presents the world in 2030 where all devices are connected (available at http://vimeo.com/31239358).

What these stories need to do is, without sensationalizing the scenario, make clear what the key ingredients of the scenario story are and describe and show what it would be like to "live" this scenario in the future.

Visualization Tools

In the last several years, visualization has gradually replaced large text documents and tables as a way of capturing the key elements of a complex story[33]. Whether it is a look at the future "breakthroughs" in science or a description of the future of e-learning, someone somewhere has created a visual representation of a complex future. Here is a cross-section of some of these:

1. **The Future of Science**: A map by the Institute for the Future (IFTF) focused on six big stories of science that will play out by

2030: Decrypting the Brain, Hacking Space, and Massively Multiplayer Data, Sea the Future, Strange Matter, and Engineered Evolution. See more at: http://newsletters.clearsignals.org/zoom_it/IFTF_SR-1454A_FutureofScience_Map_lg.jpg

2. **The Future of Health Technology**: This visualization is an exercise in speculating about which individual technologies are likely to affect the scenario of health in the coming decades. Arranged in six broad areas, the forecast covers a multitude of research and developments that are likely to disrupt the future of healthcare. Key amongst them are: regenerative medicine, augmentation using nano and information technologies, telemedicine, biogerentology, new developments in diagnosis and treatment. See more at http://envisioningtech.com/health/

3. **The Future of Educational Technology**: There are a great many developments occurring in educational applications of technology. Amongst them are adaptive assessment and learning tools, open educational resources, digital furniture and 3D Printing. See more at http://envisioningtech.com/education/

Simulators

Some tools are simple What If calculators – using established models and data, users can look at What If scenarios. For example, the Energy Futures Network in partnership with What IF Technologies developed a scenario modeling tool known as CanESS. CanESS, is a physical systems simulator that permits those engaged in energy-related futures thinking to have a reliable and robust system for entering into "what if we did this?" discussions. Others have developed similar simulators of the future of forests or the future of transport systems.

Perhaps the best known simulators to us all are weather simulators. When an extreme weather event is forecast – a hurricane, tsunami or tornado, for example – the weather forecasters use simulators to simulate the conditions which will be created and will affect the behaviour of the hurricane or tornado or tsunami. This enables emergency coordinators and planners to develop plans and contingencies for the most likely and possible scenarios. Similar simulators are used for forest fire emergency coordination and planning.

Climate change is modeled in a variety of computer simulations (over 30 of them). Each is built on a set of assumptions and uses historical data to develop climate change scenarios for the future. Whether or not these are accurate (they are clearly not at this time given that none have forecast the period of stable and cooling temperatures depending on where we are looking) we have entered into or the sudden growth of Arctic and Antarctic sea ice, all of which points to challenges with the assumptions which drive the computer models.

Games

Various military organizations use war games to explore scenarios and strategies. For example, the US military in partnership with its NATO allies use games to simulate war conditions or military action. A colleague who took part in several of these war games always found that the minute you played "outside of the box" of their normal warfare models and frameworks the enemy won (he was always asked to play the enemy leader).

In the early 1980s, I was part of a team that developed games and simulations for those training to be counseling psychologists in Wales. These simulations and games were used to challenge trainees to demonstrate competencies recently developed in workshops and training sessions. I replicated some of these when I taught briefly at Oxford.

But more recently, the advent of Gamification tools for digital devices has enabled much more elaborate simulations. For example, in the future of the economy scenario outlined briefly in Chapter 6, it would be possible to build a computer game which simulated the four scenarios and then used specific country's date (e.g. Britain) to play out a decade of economic activity, using the data from the previous 50 years and some rules for each scenario. Players would be asked at key moments to stop their "play" and explore the question: "which of the four scenarios is dominant now and what scenario is emerging as the dominant scenario?"

When training with Peter Senge and his team at MIT in systems modeling and analysis, we used a simulation of an airline (South West Airlines) as a basis for understanding the dynamics of key variables (e.g. how the decision to buy or not to buy new aircraft at key points in the game) had an impact on profitability and performance down the road. It also enabled us to develop game scenarios which later became components of the scenario models we built.

According to a study by Levine, Schelling and Jones (1991)[34], the biggest beneficiary of games are the participants but only if they consciously and systematically observe the inputs-outputs of their activities. That is, games are a serious business. Their other advice, after designing and enabling such games, is to not tell the sponsors that games were played but to focus on the outcome of playing them – what was learned in the process of game play that provides insights into the scenarios under development.

Conclusion

This chapter is more of a reminder that the process work involved in scenario planning produces a substantial volume of materials which are meaningful to those directly engaged in the process of developing strategic foresight, but which are generally inaccessible to those who are not so engaged. The challenge is to communicate the power of the foresight and scenarios through effective and focused communication tools. Video, visualization, simulation and games provide a basis for just this work.

Chapter 8: Back From the Future to Now – Getting to Strategy

Introduction

Strategic foresight is interesting work in and of itself. It is what many academics do, especially in business schools and departments of economics. There are many fascinating books looking at the future that make use of the kind of approach outlined in this short book.

But the point of strategic foresight work is to impact the strategy and action plans of organizations. If we better understood the future – both preferred and probable – should we not be able to make better strategic choices now as so as to prepare our organization or industry for that future? If we are proactive about the future, our preferred scenario is more likely to occur than if we just sit and hope that it will.

So the key value to using strategic foresight is strategy development. How do we do this?

About Strategy

In Chapter 2 we indicated that most organizations do not really know what strategy is. We defined strategy as:

> *"a determined way for an organization to differentiate itself from others operating in the same space in a way that is sustainable over time".*

That is, strategy is about creating and sustaining competitive advantage or distinctive position in a market. Most of the organizations I have encountered in over 35 years of work as a management consultant confuse strategy with planning, resource management and activity mapping.

Some elaboration of this language may be helpful to make explicit just what strategy is. Here is this statement unpicked:

- **Determined Way** – deliberate, systematic approach to strategy development and formulation.
- **Differentiate** – operate differently from others, either through "smarter" more effective business systems, customer service,

supply chains or asset management, or through a product or service offering which stands out in the market place or some combination of these features.

- **Same Space** – either same geographical space or same product space or market segment or combinations of these three.
- **Sustainable over time** – strategy is generally medium- to long-term and should persist while the key understanding of the operational context and market context remain unchanged. Strategy persists when action plans and operational plans change.

While there are many approaches to strategy formation and development, the key lies in this single statement: *How will you differentiate yourself from others offering similar products and services and sustain this difference over time?*

Strategic Choices

There are not thousands of basic strategies available to organizations. Indeed, Michael Porter suggests there are basically four generic strategies. In my book with Colin Morgan *Total Quality Management and the School*[35] we adapted Porters basic framework for public sector use[36], with a strong focus on education. The four generic strategies are based on two dimensions:

1. Market Focus – Is the organization focused on a broad market (trying to reach everyone) or on a specific niche?
2. Costs – Is the organization focused on being a least cost provider or on cost leadership?

We can explore these two dimensions in the following model of the competitive strategy space:

Target Market Space	Advantage	
	Low Cost	**Product Uniqueness**
Broad	Cost Leadership	Product Differentiation

(Wide Market for Products and Services)	Strategy	Strategy
Narrow **(Niche Market Segment)**	Focus Strategy (Least Cost Provider)	Focus Strategy (Differentiation)

Figure 8: Michael Porter's Generic Strategies

Many misunderstand the idea of cost leadership. It doesn't necessarily mean least cost provider to the consumer (though this is one option). Rather, it means that the organization can provide its products and services to the market at a low cost and therefore decide what margin of profit to secure from a sale. The iPhone, for example, carries a significant mark-up but is produced at a relatively low cost.

Let us look in a little more depth at the four generic strategies:

1. **Cost Leadership** – The strategy requires the organization to be the least cost provider of a product range or service. That is, they can deliver their product or service to market at the least cost but are able to make choices about what they charge in the market. For example, an organization can choose to offer their product or service at a very low cost so as to capture market share or at a high margin so as to secure a higher profit (and therefore attract more investment) than rivals. Organizations that seek cost leadership do so through being efficient and effective at business processes, supply chain management, the use of global systems and labour.
2. **Differentiation** – Rather than focus on cost, the organization seeks to offer products or services which are highly valued by their customers

99

or clients. Their products or services offer value-added that cannot be found in the products and services offered by others. For example, the Lexus is made by Toyota and is different from their least cost cars because it is designed for the luxury end of the car market. Such offerings usually command premium pricing. Jamie Oliver's food items, which involve premium pricing ($10 for a jar of marmalade versus $3.50 for a least cost version), are also an example of differentiation – he is targeting the global foodie market.

3. **Focus Strategy (Differentiation)** – Rather than seeking to supply products and services to a mass market, this strategy focuses on a niche within the mass market so as to ensure that it can target its products and services to the specific needs of that niche. The key challenge for this strategy is to build loyalty and commitment to the brand. In the differentiated focus strategy, there is also a focus on creating value-added products and services intended just for the niche.

4. **Focus Strategy (Least Cost)** – The fundamental concern in this strategy is to provide products and services to a niche market at the least cost and to do so relentlessly so as to beat out competitors.

Porter does suggest that there is a fifth strategy – "stuck in the middle" or, as we can also suggest, "all things to all people". What happened to General Motors (GM) was that it pursued a stuck in the middle strategy. While it built cars and trucks for the mass market and the niche markets, it managed all of its products with a relentless focus on cost control and labour constraint. The result is that it both lost market share and lost money. Porter's research (and that of many others) suggests that it is essential for the organization to choose one of the four generic strategies or, if it seeks to operate in more than one of these generic strategies, to manage each independently of the other.

Strategic Intent

We outline these four generic strategies deliberately. They are an essential starting point for understanding strategic intent.

Strategic intent is a term which describes the response to the question we asked earlier: *How will you differentiate yourself from others offering similar products and services and sustain this difference over time?* Put another way – what are the organizations intentions with respect to sustaining its competitive advantage over time? Does it intend to pursue a niche strategy or target a large market? Does it intend to be successful through differentiation or pursue a least cost strategy?

Let us explore this question in relation to school systems. In *Total Quality Management and the School*[37] we adapted Porter's generic model so as to account for the work of schools. This is what it looked like:

	Focus for Learning	
Target Student Body	**Basic Education**	**Focused on a Specialist Body of Learning (e.g. Science, Arts, Sports)**
Open to All	e.g. Comprehensive School	e.g. Community Arts School / Community Science School
Focused on a Specific Student Population	e.g. Private School or Catholic High School for Girls	e.g. Charter Arts School

Figure 9: Murgatroyd and Morgan's Generic Education Strategies (1993)

It is not suggested that one of these generic strategies is better than another or preferable to another – only that they are different from one another. A governing body and its staff need to determine which of these generic frames they are operating in. How do they intend the school to be successful?

101

Strategy as Simple Rules – The Link to Strategic Foresight

Having responded to the question – what is the strategic intent of the organization? – They then need to convert this intent into a clearer strategy. This is where the link to strategic foresight occurs. By defining the response to the rules, which we look at below, an organization translates its preferred future into strategy in a simple way.

The idea of strategy as simple rules comes from a powerful article in the Harvard Business Review in 2001 by Kathleen Eisenhardt of Stanford and Don Sull[38] of Harvard. They suggest that, having defined strategic intent, the organization should then work to describe its "how to rules" in some depth. We will outline the rules as they might apply to a school which has chosen to be a specialist arts school for those with a commitment to ballet and who pay additional fees for their ballet lessons as part of the curriculum (such a school is The School of the Alberta Ballet, though the rules outlined below do not relate to this school). These are the categories of rules they suggest need to be defined:

Type of Rule	Purpose of the Rule	Example of the Rule
How To Rules	They spell out the processes, services and activities of the organization that embody the strategic intent of the organization.	We accept pupils only on the recommendation of their ballet teacher and after an audition. All pupils will undertake ballet lessons for two hours each day, six days a week. Our advanced pupils will audition for two performances each year with the professional company.
Boundary Rules	They define the limits of the work of the	We do not accept students whose dance

	organization – indicating clearly what is "in" and "out" of scope for the work of the organization.	experience prior to admission does not involve ballet.
Priority Rules	They establish "what matters most" for the organization – what the strategically focused priorities for work should be.	Our dance focus is on traditional ballet with modern components. We aim to attract the best students in Western Canada and from Asia.
Timing Rules	They synchronize managers and leaders with the pace of change and development.	Each year, the school will commission a new ballet aimed at the 15-year-olds and it will become a "must see" performance in the ballet community in the City.
Exit Rules	They help to define when the organization should stop doing something or substantially change the way it does something.	Students who do not progress in their ballet skills year to year will be asked to leave.

Figure 10: Strategy Rules for a Ballet School

Integrating Strategic Foresight with Strategy

Having outlined the nature of strategy in terms of both generic frames and simple rules, how does an organization link strategy, rules and foresight?

First, the organization must thoroughly articulate its preferred future. It should be able to describe what that future would look and feel like for the organization. It should do so by answering these questions:

Our preferred future requires us to:

1. Develop these products
2. Offer these services
3. Recruit and retain these kinds of colleagues
4. Stop doing...
5. Improve the way we...
6. Change in a fundamental way the way we ...
7. Start doing...
8. Seek out these kinds of opportunities...
9. Work in partnership with these kinds of organizations...
10. Engage in these kinds of developments...

Having answered these questions about the preferred future (all of which arises from the scenario work already undertaken – see Chapter 6), the organization then needs to define its strategic intent and its simple strategic rules. In doing so, it may be helpful to identify what needs to change (the old rules versus the new) so as to fully begin to operate "as if" the preferred future was something the organization intends to make happen.

In *What is Strategy* (Porter, 1996)[39] Porter makes the point that all of the activities of the organization have to be aligned with the strategic intent of the organization. For example, being a least cost airline for the largest number of customers means no first class seats, no privilege meals (indeed, no meals at all) and restrictions on baggage – ask any Ryanair passenger what low cost means and they will explain it to you – "not even a thought of frills". This requires real and substantial "trade-off's" – and trade-offs need to be captured in the how to and priority rules of the organization.

Trade-offs define both what the organization does *and does not do* – with the emphasis on the latter. Trade-offs usually relate to quality, costs, time, people and the performance of the product or service. Think about schools for a moment – we could do much more in terms of (say) math education (performance of the service) with the same staff but we would have to trade-off time for other subjects and costs.

104

One way of thinking about tradeoffs is to think of what is referred to as the reality triangle:

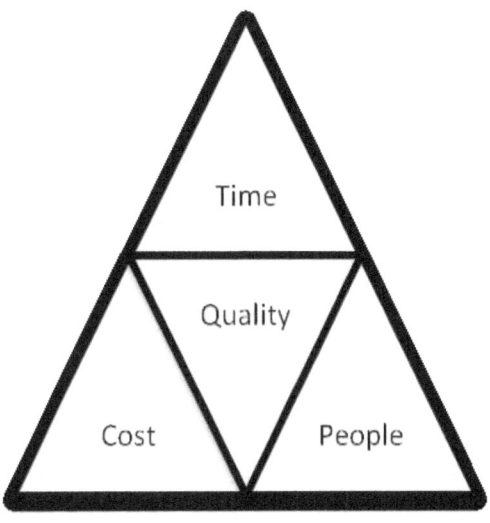

Figure 11: The Reality Triangle

All management decisions that turn strategy into action require trade-offs between these four critical points of decision. Some simplify this into three components – resources, time and scope – and others add components (e.g. functionality, depth) but the message is the same. An organization cannot do everything – it must make choices and choices involve tradeoffs. These need to be made *consciously and explicitly* in the light of the strategic intent and the strategic rules, all of which need to be related to the preferred future of the organization.

Living the Preferred Future Now

Connecting strategy to strategic foresight really requires the organization to begin to operate "as if" its preferred future was the one it is working to make happen without losing the "as if" quality of this work.

Part of the reasons for highlighting the "as if" quality of this work is that many of those the organization is dealing with will be unaware of the future scenarios the organization has developed. They will still be operating as if the future is a straight line from the past. It will take time to engage and persuade those not involved in the work on strategic foresight and strategy development to "own" a different future.

Nonetheless, the sooner the organization begins to live its preferred future the more likely it is to happen – we explore this in more depth in the last Chapter of this book. If you need an example, look at the history of Apple – a corporation once "written off" and in decline that turned itself around with the development of its suite of mobile devices. These devices are the direct result of some powerful foresight and strategy work undertaken within Apple.

Conclusion

Without this link to strategy, strategic foresight carries the danger of being "of interest" and "valuable". With this link to strategy, strategic foresight becomes an engine of change and development within the organization. It is no accident that the work of Royal Dutch Shell on strategic foresight came from its Group Planning department under the guidance of its then leader, Pierre Wack. Shell didn't just look at the scenario's Wack developed, it acted on them. In doing so, it moved from being the smallest of the seven major oil companies to the second in size and number one in profitability – it adopted its preferred future as the starting point for its strategy and acted accordingly, making trade-offs that aligned with its strategic intent.

Chapter 9: Utilizing a Challenge Dialogue – Focus and Alignment Through Engagement

Introduction

In the previous chapter we noted that many working within an organization and with an organization will be unaware of the strategic foresight work it has conducted and the strategy and trade-off decisions which will have resulted from it. As those who have been involved begin to "roll out" their preferred future and act accordingly, they will find it difficult to fully comprehend what is taking place and, more importantly, why.

In this chapter, we introduce a tool developed by Don Simpson and Keith Jones for the Innovation Expedition that is designed to respond to this situation. It provides a basis for engaging a large number of people in understanding the different future the organization is working towards and its implications and to do so efficiently and simply. It is also a tool for securing alignment within an organization and those who are directly engaged with it. The tool is called a Challenge Dialogue.

What the Challenge Dialogue Process Seeks to Do

A challenge dialogue seeks to document clearly and explicitly:

- The circumstances and events which have led to change and the dialogue – why is there a need to focus on change and development?
- The key assumptions being made – for example, assumptions about the trends and drivers which require the organization to change, assumptions about the scenarios which the strategic foresight work has developed.
- The implications of these assumptions for the strategy of the organization – what has to change?
- The implications of these changes for the strategic rules of the organization.
- The implications of these changes for different groups and teams within the organization.

In laying out these things clearly and directly, individuals are asked if they are aligned with the assumptions and changes outlined therein and also to provide feedback so that the thinking can be continuously improved.

The process helps to focus a large group of people and secure their alignment with the preferred future of the organization.

The process also intends to be a significant contribution to building a community of like-minded and engaged organizational members and to develop organizational resilience. Given that, especially in large organizations, not everyone can share the work of strategic foresight; this process helps to engage the broader organizational community and its stakeholders.

When To Use A Challenge Dialogue

There are a variety of points in a strategic foresight expedition that a Challenge Dialogue process could be used. For example, it may be helpful to conduct a challenge dialogue at the stage between trend and pattern development and building scenarios so as to see if the organization – especially those nearest the customer – sees trends and patterns that others have missed. When we did this with a retail company the front line staff we engaged identified a key trend – the growing number of demanding customers – a trend the top team had missed.

It may also be appropriate between the completion of the scenario process and the work on connecting the preferred scenario to strategy to engage a wider group in a challenge dialogue.

When it is essential is when the organization leadership has built the bridge between the preferred scenario and its strategic intent and rules so as to ensure that there is focus and alignment across the organization with the new direction and its implications.

How To Develop A Challenge Document

A small team needs to engage in a serious conversation about what should be in the core document that a broad group of people will be asked to respond to. The following are our usual headings when a challenge dialogue is being used for strategic foresight:

The Purpose of This Document

- A brief outline of the structure of the document and its purpose.
- A call for responses by a certain date.

- An explanation of how responses can be provided – online, by email, by telephone or in-person (if appropriate).

Events Which Have Led to This Dialogue

- A catalogue of critical events that suggest the need to change.
- A small number (3-5) of case vignettes (150-200 words) that illustrate the need to change in a concrete way.

Critical Assumptions About the Future

- A list of key trends, patterns and wild cards identified in the strategic foresight process with some evidence.
- An outline of the basic scenario frameworks.
- A list of implications of the changing future as a result of these scenarios and trends.

The Preferred Future

- A statement of the preferred future for the organization.
- The risks of the future not being the preferred future.
- The implications of the preferred future.

Strategic Intent and Rules

- So as to make the preferred future possible, here is a statement of our strategic intent.
- This strategic intent leads to these strategic rules.
- These strategic rules have these consequences – what we need to stop doing, improve, redesign and start.

– in other words, the document captures the strategic foresight expedition's key findings. It needs to do so succinctly and economically, but do so in such a way as to make explicit the key elements of the thinking that point to the need for change.

At each section of the document, those receiving it are asked to provide feedback and their response. But the "ask" is done in a particular way. We ask:

1. Is there anything in this section that needs further explanation for clarity?

2. Is there anything missing from this section which you think is important for us to understand and integrate into our thinking and planning?
3. Are you aligned with the statements in this section? If not, why not?

The aim is to engage in a meaningful dialogue. Responses can be anonymous, but it is preferable for individuals to be identified to the outfitters as part of the process – they can be assured that their names will not appear in any reports resulting from this process.

You can modify these headings and questions for the specific situation in which you find yourself. You may also wish to conduct a challenge dialogue in stages – stage one on trends and scenarios; stage two on strategy and strategic rules, for example. The process needs to be adapted to the situation in which you find yourself.

We have made use of technology to support this process, though the process also works well with paper and email. A simple web design (for example, www.albertapulpandpaper.ca) was used to engage a large community in looking at the future of the pulp and paper industry in a particular jurisdiction. We have also used www.surveymonkey.com to secure easy to analyze feedback from an organization, for example looking at the future of the bioeconomy in a particular jurisdiction. We have also used telephone "phone-ins" (for example, an hour slot for all Municipal Mayors with pulp mills in their districts) which was audio-recorded and notes taken at the time to secure feedback. The more options people have to give feedback, the more active listening the organization can engage in.

What We Heard Document

When all the responses are returned, the outfitters then go to work to summarise responses. They develop a *What We Heard* document which captures the feedback. The aim of this document is to provide assurance to all engaged in this process that their voices are being heard.

In this same document, the Champions are also asked to give their response to the feedback. For example, if there are real issues with the way in which the preferred future is outlined, the Champions may clarify, expand and add to the description of the preferred future so that it is clear.

The What We Heard document is then sent to everyone who was asked to participate in the challenge dialogue whether or not they responded.

Challenge Dialogue (Version 2)

The feedback is often substantial from a challenge dialogue. For example, in a dialogue focused on the strategy aimed at reducing the incidence of heart and stroke disease in Alberta and increasing survival rates for those who experience a heart attack or a stroke, over 170 responses were received from a pool of 190 respondents in just ten days – each response providing rich feedback which caused the Champions to look again at some key aspects of the original challenge dialogue document.

As a result of the feedback, the Champions and Outfitters look at the original challenge dialogue document and make decisions about what, if anything, needs to be changed. For example, all of the requests for clarification and clarity need to be addressed; suggestions about items to be included need to be considered and objections to the way in which the future is presented (whether in terms of strategies, strategic rules or implications) need to be thought through. The new document which reflects these considerations is then sent out again for comment and feedback – one final time. The request for feedback may be modified – does this now fully reflect the views documented in "What We Heard?" may be a question, for example. But the point is that the process makes clear that change is going to occur.

This process enables all engaged to see the impact their suggestions have, see change occurring and see a learning organization in action. This is a way to build focus and alignment and to secure commitment across an organization.

Base Camp

Sometimes, especially if version 1 of the challenge document suggests key areas in which there are strong issues and lack of alignment in the organization, there is a need to call a meeting of key people, including dissenters, to discuss their concerns. While it would be good to secure agreement – the key task is to secure understanding and alignment.

Such a base camp can be difficult. Imagine 150 oil executives from 43 different companies trying to agree on the future shape of their industry in a particular jurisdiction – it is not easy to secure alignment. What we tried for, in this example, is shared understanding and identifying those areas in which there was alignment and those areas in which we agreed to disagree but also agreed to continue to work together.

The Value of a Challenge Dialogue

The Challenge Dialogue System™ (CDS) has been used in a great many contexts and for a great many different reasons. There are short and long versions of this process, two year dialogues and two month dialogues. Here are the benefits we have discerned:

- Fast and efficient way of securing feedback, focus and alignment from a large number of people who have commitments to the issue at hand.
- Comprehensive way of documenting all of the concerns that arise in a single place (What we Heard) and showing how these have an impact on thinking and planning (Challenge Dialogue version 2).
- A way of quickly understanding the issues of concern to influencers and key players in the organization – concerns that need to be addressed (Base Camp).
- A way of understanding what needs to be clarified – how ambiguity can get in the way of understanding – and an opportunity to clarify so that understanding can be clearer (Challenge Dialogue version 2).
- Flexible – the process and system can be adapted to the context and circumstances.

Our experience, for example in a national dialogue on innovation policy and strategy for all of the Canadian Provinces and Territories, is that it is the assumptions that create the most "buzz" in this process. Where there is little or no agreement that the Champions and outfitters have understood the situation – revealed through the assumptions and trend analysis – then all else "fails". Most feedback will concern assumptions and trends.

The downside of this work is that it involves "risk". One Deputy Minister of a major Federal department was worried that the "What We Heard" document might reveal the degree of dissent within her own Department and that this constituted a risk. It was a risk she took, but she was, in part, right – the process revealed that the core assumptions used to rethink several key policies were overly restricted and that when we added six other assumptions that "screamed" at us from the feedback the strategy and action plans changed. The

112

Department was stronger, more focused and aligned than might have otherwise been the case and, rather than being weakened by this, the Deputy Minister's position was strengthened by her demonstrating active listening and proactive change.

The other weakness relates not so much to the process but to the follow-through. This process has produced great success and many notable outcomes, but it is about the way in which the Champions take the results of the process and act upon them. The process can create a launch pad, but for the "take off" to occur the Champions have to be willing to stay with the journey.

Conclusion

We present this process as an opportunity to communicate and engage many more people across the organization and more of the organization's stakeholders in a strategic foresight journey – as a way of broadening the base of support for the strategy and actions which fall out of the work of a strategic foresight expedition. The CDS process is adaptable and flexible.

Chapter 10: Making the Preferred Future Now – Action For Change

Introduction
In chapters two to nine we have described the nature of a strategic foresight expedition – the "how to". We have shown the key stages and outlined some of the techniques and approaches to the work of strategic foresight. We have shown how to link scenarios to strategy and how to convert strategic intent into specific rules which show the organization what strategy has to look like. In this final chapter, we describe what the organization has to do to demonstrate its commitment to its own preferred future

Strategic Foresight as a Change Management Process
John Kotter has developed a simple, but effective, framework for change management which speaks to the way in which the work of a strategic foresight expedition connects to the need for an organization to start to make its preferred future its basis for action. The Kotter model involves eight steps, shown in the simple figure below.

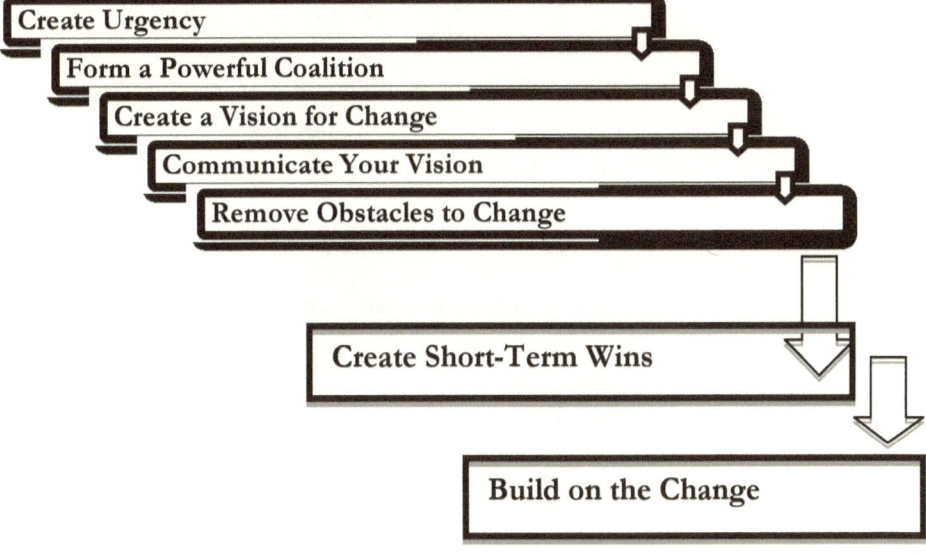

Figure 12: Kotter's Change Models

We present Kotter's model – there are literally hundreds of change models available – since it speaks directly to the very nature of a strategic foresight expedition. Now let us look at how this model helps us understand the expedition we are engaged in.

Step 1: Create Urgency
For change to happen, it helps if the whole company really wants it. The strategic foresight process – especially mapping alternative futures based on uncertainties from the trend and pattern analysis, should help to develop a sense of urgency around the need for change. This may help spark the initial motivation to get things moving but also help things to move in the direction of the preferred future.

This isn't simply a matter of showing people poor sales statistics or talking about increased competition. Open an honest and convincing dialogue about what is happening in the world – shown by your in-depth review of trends, patterns and wild cards, enables a new and different conversation. If many people start talking about the change needed, the urgency can build and feed on itself.

From experience, we work to sell the need to change before we start to focus on just what the preferred future might be. That is, understanding that the future isn't a straight line from the past but that there are disruptions ahead and change ahead is important. Urgency comes not from fear (though this can sometimes help, but not always) – it is more likely to come from understanding uncertainty.

What you can do:
- Identify potential threats, and develop scenarios showing what could happen in the future – the key to strategic foresight work.
- Examine opportunities that should be, or could be, exploited and document them and the assumptions behind them – a challenge dialogue can help with this work.
- Start honest discussions, and give dynamic and convincing reasons to get people talking and thinking – this is exactly what the challenge dialogue process does.
- Request support from customers, outside stakeholders and industry people to strengthen your argument – get them to

understand and add evidence to the trend analysis and show that some of the signals for the scenarios under consideration can now be seen.

Kotter suggests that for change to be successful, 75% of a company's leadership and management needs to "buy into" the change. In other words, Step 1 is a critical step and the more you can engage the leadership of the organization in the strategic foresight process, the more likely the change is to occur. Spend significant time and energy building urgency, before moving onto the next steps. Don't panic and jump in too fast because you don't want to risk further short-term losses – if you act without proper preparation, you could be in for a very bumpy ride. This is why strategic foresight relies heavily on the trend / pattern and wildcard stage on evidence and data. Show that the outfitters and champions really do understand what is happening and have evidence to show for it.

Step 2: Form a Powerful Coalition
Convince people that change is necessary. This often takes strong leadership and visible support from key people within your organization. Managing change isn't enough – you have to lead it. This is why developing a very clear preferred future statement which has consequences is important – it is a guiding resource to focus change. This is also why the work on linking strategic foresight to strategy is so important – the strategic intent, strategic rules and implications have to be thoroughly thought through before "launch" so that all in the organization can make the connection between the "rules", the proposed changes and the preferred future. If this connection is weak, you could delay change by a considerable period of time.

You can find effective change leaders throughout your organization – they don't necessarily follow the traditional company hierarchy. To lead change, you need to bring together a coalition, or team, of influential people whose power comes from a variety of sources, including job title, status, expertise, and political importance.

Once formed, your "change coalition" needs to work as a team, continuing to build urgency and momentum around the need for change. The Champions and outfitters together with those who have been engaged in the strategic foresight journey are key to this work. Bu they may not be enough – use the challenge dialogue process to identify new change Champions at all levels of the organization.

What you can do:
- Identify the true leaders in your organization, not just by status but by influence and engage them from the get-go in the strategic foresight expedition (see Chapter 3 above).
- Ask for an emotional commitment from these key people – ask them to bring their whole self to the table, not just their sharp brains and wit.
- Work on team building within your change coalition – use the Team Charter (Chapter 3) and the trend / pattern work (Chapter 4) to really build a powerful, mindful and committed team.
- Check your team for weak areas, and ensure that you have a good mix of people from different departments and different levels within your organization – make sure all voices are represented.

Step 3: Create a Vision for Change
Develop scenarios and the work on linking these to strategy should help create a powerful sense of what the organization needs to become. The statement of the preferred future is a visionary statement about what the organization needs to become – a statement of strategic intent. The organizational rules which accompany this make clear that this is not just a "vision thing" but is, in fact, a statement of what the organization will do to make its preferred future happen.

A clear and explicit preferred future statement can help everyone understand why you are asking them to do something and what you are asking them to do. When people see for themselves what you are trying to achieve, then the directives they are given tend to make more sense. Using a challenge dialogue to enable them to engage, focus and align helps them see the what, why and how of the change the preferred future calls for.

What you can do:
- Determine the values that are central to the change.
- Develop a concise, focused, preferred future statement.
- Create a strategy to execute that vision – show the connection between the preferred future, strategic intent and strategic rules.
- Ensure that your change coalition can describe the vision in five minutes or less.

- Practice the "preferred future speech" often.
- Use a challenge dialogue to engage the entire organization in understanding the preferred future and its implications.

Step 4: Communicate the Vision

What you do with your preferred future after you create it will determine your success. Your message will probably have strong competition from other day-to-day activities, challenges and communications within the organization, so you need to communicate it frequently and powerfully, and embed it within everything that you do. This is where visualization and video can play a powerful part (see Chapter 7).

Don't just call special meetings to communicate the preferred future. Instead, talk about it every chance you get. Use a challenge dialogue to communicate it. Find different ways to embed it in the work of the organization at the team and unit level. When you keep it fresh on everyone's minds, they'll remember it and respond to it.

It is also important to "walk the talk." What you do is far more important – and believable – than what you say. Demonstrate the kind of behaviour that you want from others – the kind of behaviour represented by the strategic rules which also represent the preferred future in action.

What you can do:
- Talk often about the preferred future.
- Openly and honestly address peoples' concerns and anxieties – refer back to the trends, patterns, wild cards and scenarios when you do so. Use evidence.
- Apply the preferred future to all aspects of operations – from training to performance reviews. Tie everything back to the statement of what the future needs to look like.
- Lead by example.

Step 5: Remove Obstacles

If you follow these steps and reach this point in the change process, you have been building buy-in from all levels of the organization to the preferred future and the strategies which accompanies it. Hopefully, your colleague's want to get busy and achieve the benefits that you have been promoting and lead the future through action, not words.

But is anyone resisting the change? And are there processes or structures that are getting in its way? From experience, especially in the public sector, the answer will be "yes".

Put in place a team for change and task them with the identification of barriers to change. Ask them to first understand the barrier – is it rejecting or slowing change towards the preferred future for a good reason (often the case) or just because it fears loss of authority, power and control? Just steamrolling over barriers is a mistake – there is a need to understand them and appreciate the concerns and develop case-by-case approaches to overcoming them.

Removing obstacles and barriers to the preferred future can take time, but can also empower and enable the people you need to make the preferred future come alive, and it can help the needed changes move forward.

What you can do:
- Identify, or hire, change leaders whose main roles are to deliver the change.
- Look at your organizational structure, job descriptions, and performance and compensation systems to ensure they are in line with your preferred future.
- Recognize and reward people for making change happen.
- Identify people who are resisting the change, and help them see what is needed.
- Take action to quickly remove barriers (human or otherwise), based on an understanding of what the barrier is, why it is there and what the opportunity of removing the barrier represents.

Tip: Not all barriers are equal. You need to pick off those that "matter most "since they represent major obstacles to the preferred future.

Step 6: Create Short-Term Wins
Nothing motivates more than success. Give your organization a taste of victory early on in the change process. Within a short time frame (this could be a month or a year, depending on the type and scale of change); you will want to have results that your staff can see. Without this, critics and negative thinkers might hurt your progress. These results should be linked to the scenario signposts that relate to your preferred future.

Create short-term goals and targets and goals that demonstrate that the organization is "on track" for its preferred future. Do not rely on just one long-term goal. You want each smaller goal to be achievable, with little room for failure. Your change team may have to work very hard to come up with these targets, but each "win" that you produce can further motivate the entire staff. Celebrate each "win" and communicate these widely.

What you can do:
- Look for sure-fire projects that you can implement without help from any strong critics of the change that show that the preferred future is "happening now".
- Don't choose early targets that are expensive. You want to be able to justify the investment in each project.
- Thoroughly analyze the potential pros and cons of your targets. If you don't succeed with an early goal, it can hurt your entire change initiative.
- Reward the people who help you meet the targets.

Step 7: Build on the Change
John Kotter argues that many change projects fail because victory is declared too early – think of George Bush on the back of the aircraft carrier USS; Abraham Lincoln declaring victory in Iraq and the start of a "new era" on May 2nd, 2003 – almost a decade too early. Real change runs deep and takes time. Quick wins are only the beginning of what needs to be done to achieve long-term change aimed at ensuring that the preferred future is the one the organization delivers.

Launching one new product using a new system is great. But if you can launch 10 such products, that means the new system is working. To reach that 10th success, you need to keep looking for improvements. Each success provides an opportunity to build on what went right and identify what you can improve upon.

In a bioindustrial strategy development, to use a different example, it is not implementing the strategy that counts, it is seeing companies and organizations utilizing the strategy to develop new products and services and build a powerful bioeconomy which employs more and more people and contributes more each year to the GDP of a jurisdiction that counts. It is seeing the bioeconomy contributes to the reduction of the carbon footprint of a jurisdiction that counts.

What you can do:
- After every win or achievement, analyze what went right and what needs improving and act to enable these developments across the organization.
- Set goals to continue building on the momentum towards the preferred future that has been achieved.
- Learn about the idea of continuous improvement (Kaizen) and six sigma and start to use these skills and tools to make change sustainable.
- Keep ideas fresh by bringing in new change agents and leaders for your change coalition.
- Celebrate success often and communicate success all the time.
- Use visualization and video to capture the change (before and after) and connect the building blocks of change to the preferred future and strategic intent of the organization.

Step 8: Anchor the Changes in Corporate Culture

Finally, to make any change stick, it should become part of the core of your organization. Your corporate culture often determines what gets done, so the values behind your vision must show in day-to-day work. Keep the preferred future in the minds of all in the organization by embedding its implications in the work of each team.

Make continuous efforts to ensure that the change is seen in every aspect of your organization. This will help give that change a solid place in your organization's culture.

It is also important that your company's leaders continue to support the change in work and behaviour linked to the preferred future. This includes existing staff and new leaders who are brought in. If you lose the support of these people, you might end up back where you started.

What you can do:
- Talk about progress every chance you get. Tell success stories about the change process, and repeat other stories that you hear. Link these stories to the preferred future and develop signposts (visually) that

show the organization is on track for delivering the preferred future now.

- Include the change ideals and values when hiring and training new staff. Make them talk about the preferred future during the hiring process.
- Publicly recognize key members of your original change coalition, and make sure the rest of the staff – new and old – remembers their contributions.
- Create plans to replace key leaders of change as they move on. This will help ensure that their legacy is not lost nor forgotten.

Conclusion

You have to work hard to change an organization successfully as a result of a strategic foresight expedition. When you plan carefully and build the proper foundation, implementing change can be much easier, and you will improve the chances of success. If you are too impatient, and if you expect too many results too soon, your plans for change are more likely to fail. The solid work required during a strategic foresight expedition lays the foundation for effective change and development. It also builds the basic coalition needed to make the preferred future happen.

Create a sense of urgency, recruit powerful change leaders, build a preferred future and effectively communicate the strategy. Such a coalition of smart leaders can remove obstacles, secure quick wins, and build on the momentum created during the foresight expedition. If this work is done well the Champions and outfitters can help make the change part of your organizational culture. That is when you can declare that the preferred future has arrived.

It is usually then time to start the process all over again.

Back Pack and Tool Box

In the pages that follow some tools and guides are provided to support your strategic foresight expedition. They are provided as a resource and will each require adaptation for effective use in the particular situation you are engaged in. All strategic foresight expeditions are different – there is no tool kit purpose built for the challenge you are engaged in. Each time, you will need to adopt and adapt resources to meet the challenge of your expedition.

We use the stages of the expedition as a framework for presenting these tools.

Step 1: Preparing for the Foresight Expedition

Tool 1: A Team Charter

In Chapter 3, we outlined the need for the strategic foresight team to develop a team charter. Below we provide a template for this work.

Teams work better if the members are united to a common purpose and everyone is clear about their roles and expectations. Having a name (and possibly a logo) and a mission statement helps build unity, while defining roles and ground rules lets everyone know where they stand minimizing the risk of conflict and facilitating task completion. A team member skills inventory helps identify the strengths and weaknesses of the members, which may save time in assigning and accomplishing group tasks. Setting goals and being aware of potential obstacles to their achievement – a skill central to the management process – encourages teams to develop contingency plans and take an active approach to problem identification and problem solving. An essential element of a good team charter is conflict resolution mechanisms. Conflict cannot – and probably should not – be completely avoided, but it can and should be managed. By identifying the likely kinds of issues that might bring team members into conflict and agreeing beforehand how to deal constructively with those conflicts, team members will help to ensure the optimum functioning of the team. One common conflict, for example, is the perception that one or more team members are not doing a fair share of the work. This can be the result of unclear or conflicting expectations, or of an intentional or unavoidable failure to follow through on assignments or attendance. Either way, by agreeing on the "rules of engagement" before conflicts even arise, teams can manage it more ably should it arise.

Team Name:

Team Mission and Objectives or Goals
- Begin with a one or two sentence statement of what the team is supposed to do.

Why your team exists
- What are you trying to accomplish in general terms?

- The specific goals and or outcomes that you are hoping to achieve over the life of the team. These include but are not limited to:

- Objectives relating to task completion

- Objectives relating to task quality

- The development of specific team "process" skills

- Members should also identify barriers that may hinder goal attainment (e.g. work commitments, not understanding the work required, failing to adhere to ground rules, etc.).

- These goals and objectives need not be limited to the course project. E.g. You may want to help each other prepare for exams.

Team Member Skill Inventory
- Team members can identify for the others what they think they bring to the team in terms of the task and maintenance roles they can fulfill.
- You can also identify any skills or knowledge areas they would like to work on during the team process and to solicit the help of others.

Role Identification
What are the different roles that members of the team will take on to support its success? These can be permanently assigned or rotated. Examples include:
- Leader
- Chairperson
- Facilitator
- Scribe/Secretary
- Communications coordinator
- Resource person/Technical support
- Editor

Ground Rules
The basic values and operating principles and procedures that will govern your life as a team. They may include such things as:
- **Assignments**
  - Assigning responsibilities
  - Setting deadlines
  - Meeting deadlines
  - Quality of work
- **Meetings**
  - Attendance Expectations
  - Schedules/Times

- Locations
- Coming Prepared
- Protocol
- Agendas
- Notifications
- Record keeping

- **Attitude**

- **Contacting**

    - Method (email, phone, on-line, etc.)
    - Limits
- **What will serve as acceptable excuses?**

- **Penalties**

- **How will you control the master copy of the report?**

- **How will decisions be made within the group?**

Conflict Resolution Mechanisms

- What are potential sources of conflict and how will you deal with them?

- e.g. All problems will be kept within the group until that is no longer a solution and then we must go to the higher authority.

Preliminary Project Plan

Once the foundation for a successful team has been laid, team members can then begin to plan for the accomplishment of its course project by working on a preliminary project plan. This should include things such as:

- identification of tasks or processes

- member assignments

- due dates

Performance criteria

Five performance Criteria, with descriptions, must be prepared and included in the charter. See the information on Peer Evaluations.

Sign Off:

I have participated in the development of this charter and agree to it.

Team Member: _____

Team Member: _____

Team Member: _____

Team Member: _____

Date:

Tool 2: The Crossroads Issues Tool

This is a tool used to begin a strategic review process – the starting point for strategic foresight. We are asking: what are the issues that are so important we have to look to the future and rethink strategy? In short: we're at a crossroads and we need to really think about what we are doing.

Step 1: Top Ten List

Make a list of the issues that are seen by the team as "crossroad issues". Describe them. You don't want hundreds of issues – we normally settle on the top ten. Here is a simple way of capturing them:

Issue	Description
1	
2	
3	
4	
5	

Step 2: Reviewing the Crossroad

Having ascertained the top ten list, now we need to agree what really matters here. Here is an approach to this work:

1. For each issue assess how urgent it is – use a 5 point scale where 5 is really urgent.
2. For each issue assess how important it is – again a simple 5 point scale helps. Remember – an issue can be urgent (we have to sort out car parking) but it may not be all that important when we take a long term view of the organization or challenge.
3. Now look again at each issue and ask, "how solvable is this?" Some are solvable – with resources and focus. Other issues may be very difficult to solve. Use the same scoring system – 5 for almost impossible to solve.
4. Taking into account the urgency, importance and solvability into account, rank the issues – those that are both really urgent, very important, and difficult to solve get the highest rank. These are the key crossroad issues.

You can use this simple table to help this work:

Issue	Urgency	Importance	Solvability	Rank
1				
2				
3				
4				
5				

Step 3: Current State Assessment

Tool 3: The Seven S's

We described the Seven S's briefly in Chapter 2. The tool was developed by Lowell Bryan at McKinsey's New York office in the late 1970s. It asks you to look cold and hard at the organization (or profession or industry) in terms of seven key variables that shape performance and outcomes. The key is to remember that these are seven variables that interact – a change in one affects the other six. Ask the team these questions (where we say organization, it could be institution, profession, industry sector):

The Variable	The Question
Strategy	Is the strategy we are pursuing clear to all and owned by all and is the right strategy for the next decade?
Style	When others experience our organization, what is that experience like? Do we have a distinctive style, presence and brand? Is this style fit for purpose and will it sustain us for the next decade?
Skills	Do we have the right skill sets in all areas of our organization? Are these the skills that will sustain us for the next decade?
Systems	Are our systems (HR systems, financial systems, supply chain logistics, customer facing systems, communications) the best they can be in enabling innovation, responsiveness and performance?
Structure	Does the structure of this organization enable us to move quickly, nimbly and effectively in response to changed conditions? Does our structure inhibit our innovative and adaptive capacity?
Staff	Do we have the right people in the right place doing the right things?
Shared Values	Do our people share a set of values and aspirations for this organization and does doing so create a culture of commitment and performance unique in this industry sector?

Tool 4: SWOT and SCORE

SWOT Analysis

SWOT (strengths, weaknesses, opportunities and threats) is another approach to exploring the current state of an organization, profession, industry or network. The idea is simple: We build a collaborative understanding – preferably with an evidence base for each proposition under each heading – this captures the current state (strengths and weaknesses) and the challenges and opportunities the organization faces.

We can think of this as a set of questions. Here are some to get us going:

What are your organisation's strengths and weaknesses?

- What are your main achievements over the last three years?
- How successful have you been in achieving your strategic objectives?
- Have you met or exceeded your targets?
- Do your current services meet users' requirements?
- How effective are your links with other key organisations /agencies in your area or sector?
- How secure is your organisation's financial position?
- Do you have the staffing levels and expertise necessary to meet your objectives?
- How is your organisation regarded externally?
- Does it have a good reputation? Are you able to build effective relationships with those you wish to influence?
- Do you have a positive relationship with your funders/supporters?
- Is your organisation effective at communicating with external groups?
- How effective are your management systems and processes? Is your organisation well-structured and efficient or overly bureaucratic?
- Does your management / leadership team have the capacity/expertise to meet the demands of the organisation?

What are the key opportunities and threats facing your organisation?

- Trends in your area of work/services •
- Audit of local situation
- Membership / User needs
- Demographics
- Competition from other or similar organisations in your area
- Facilities
- Barriers to your organisation's development
- Deprivation of your catchment area, e.g. Noble Deprivation Indices
- Consultation findings, e.g. community audit, needs assessment, etc

- Opportunities for developing new area of work – Opportunities for extending services to new audiences
- Partnerships / Collaborative working opportunities
- Central Government policies and regulations (present and pending)

Team members develop evidence-based responses to these (and related) questions so as to build a picture of the current state.

SCORE Analysis

A more contemporary approach to this same work makes use of a different framework: Strengths, Challenges, Options, Responses and Effectiveness (SCORE). This leads us to explore different questions:

Our Strengths

- Strengths
  - What would we regard as our strengths in this?
- Services
  - What services and capabilities do we have?
  - What services can we call on from others?
- Support
  - What support-resources do we have available to us?
  - What support do we have, from others?

Our Challenges

- Challenges
  - What are the issues we need to address?
    - within the organization
    - in relationships with partners, suppliers, other stakeholders?
- Capabilities needed
  - What new capabilities and services would we need?

- o What skills would be required?

- o What would be needed to develop these skills and services?

Our Options

- Opportunities

  - o What opportunities present themselves?

  - o What risks arise from with those opportunities?

  - o What opportunities arise from apparent risks?

- Options

  - o What are our options in relation to those opportunities and risks?

  - o How can we act on those options?

  - o How should we prioritize those options and actions?

Our Responses

- Responses

  - o What responses would we expect from other stakeholders?

    - ▪ from customers? competitors? providers? partners?

- Regulations

  - o What regulations might arise in response to our strategy?

  - o What would be the impacts of new or upcoming legislation?

- Returns / Rewards

  - o What is the business value of each opportunity and risk?

Our Efficiency

- Is it Efficient?

  - o maximizes use of resources, minimizes wastage of resources

- Is it Reliable?

  - o predictable, consistent, self-correcting

- Is it Elegant?

  - o clarity, simplicity, consistency, self-adjusting for human factors

- Is it Appropriate?

  - o supports and maximizes support for business purpose

- Is it Integrated?

  - o creates, supports and maximizes synergy across all systems

Again, the expectation is that the team working on the expedition would document and produce evidence for an analysis of the current state in response to these questions.

Tool 5: Six Forces Analysis

Michael Porter, formerly of the Harvard Business School, developed an approach to industry analysis and competitive analysis which made use of some basic economics of how industries function. He suggested that we should explore these factors:

- **Competition** – A systematic assessment of the direct competitors in a given market.
- **New Entrants** - A systematic assessment of the potential competitors and barriers to entry in a given market.
- **End Users/ Buyers** - A systematic assessment regarding the bargaining power of buyers that includes considering the cost of switching to other suppliers or alternative products or services.
- **Suppliers** - A systematic assessment regarding the bargaining power of suppliers across the whole supply chain and an understanding of the challenges associated with supply chain logistics.
- **Substitutes** – A thoroughgoing and realistic assessment regarding the availability of alternative products or services.
- **Complementary Products** - A systematic assessment of the impact of related products and services within a given market.

The key to this work is not to be defensive about the current state but to be realistic and honest about what is and what could be.

Tool 6: Moments of Truth (MoT) Matrix

The term 'Moment of Truth' was coined by Jan Carlzon, who was CEO of Scandinavian SAS Airlines. He used the term to mean those moments in which important brand impressions are formed and where there is significant opportunity for good or bad impressions to be made. Moments of Truth often happen when they are not thought to occur, in odd interfaces with staff and moments with products. When customers have certain expectations and they are disappointed, then they can form very negative impressions or feel a sense of betrayal that sends them into destructive desires for retribution. A bad customer moment of truth leads the customer to tell up to 10 other people about it; an excellent moment of truth may simply be regarded as normal and not worth sharing.

We use this as a way of understanding how our organization is experienced by customers (or suppliers). We ask: what are the top 10 moments of truth for customers of this organization – moments at which our reputation is "on the line" for them? For airline passengers, such a moment can be how lost bags are handled or overbooking is managed. For hotel guests, how poor room service is managed. For a financial institution, how a wrongly recorded financial transaction or identify theft is handled.

This is important, since it captures how well the organization is at anticipating customer needs, creating systems to support these needs and empowering staff to handle these issues nearest to the customer.

Here is a way of capturing the work you need to do – best done through exploring with customers in focus groups or through survey data.

MoT		Description		Organizational Impact		Customer Impact	
		Costs	Revenue	Service	Brand	Customer Retention	Customer Recommendations
1	e.g. Lost	H	L	H	M	M	H

	Bags						
2							
3							
4							

For each of the organizational and customer impact categories, we look at high/medium/low impacts. We really want to know what the costs of a moment of truth (e.g. lost baggage are), what revenue opportunities may exist from offering service guarantees, what impact the MoT has on our brand and service provision – is there an opportunity to rethink this MoT to make it a brand-building revenue opportunity? On the customer side, we want to know if the MoT adversely affects customer behaviour – retention and their willingness to recommend our company to a friend or colleague.

Step 3: Finding Common Ground: Trends and Patterns
Chapter 5 outlines some of the key practices for identifying trends and patterns. There are a growing number of online tools to explore trends and patterns. Here are the top 10:

- Google Trends – Google Search Trends
- adCenter Search Volume Seasonality Trends
- adCenter Keyword Forecast
- Facebook Lexicon – Facebook Social Trends
- Twist – Trends in Twitter
- Trendpedia – Blog Trends
- BlogPulse from Nielsen – Another Blog Trends Tool
- Trendrr – Trends across Social Graphs and Networks
- Google Checkout Trends – Online Sales Trends
- Indeed Job Trends Tool

We can also use more traditional methods – focus groups, Delphi and analysis of data (e.g. demographic data, financial and economic data, health analytics, etc.).

Tool 7: Delphi Process

A traditional method of strategic foresight is the Delphi process. Here we use a group of experts in a field in which we are interested in and ask them to agree to participate in a multi-stage process. This process looks like this:

Step 1: Choose a Facilitator

The first step is to choose your facilitator. You may wish to take on this role yourself, or find a *'neutral'* person within your organization. It is useful to have someone that is familiar with research and data collection.

Step 2: Identify Your Experts

The Delphi technique relies on a panel of experts. This panel may be your project team, including the customer, or other experts from within your organization or industry. An expert is "any individual with relevant knowledge and experience of a particular topic."

Step 3: Define the Problem

What is the problem or issue you are seeking to understand? The experts need to understand exactly what they are commenting on, so ensure you provide a clear and comprehensive definition.

Step 4: Round One Questions

Ask general questions to gain a broad understanding of the views of the experts about future events. The questions may go out in the form of questionnaires or surveys. Collated and summarize the responses removing any irrelevant content and look for common viewpoints. For example, you might ask, "What six issues will dominate the next 10 years of educational change and development and why do you think these six are the most important?"

Step 5: Round Two Questions

Based on the answers to the first questions, these questions should delve deeper into the topic to clarify specific issues. These questions may also go out in the form of questionnaires or surveys. Again, collate and summarize the results removing any irrelevant content and look for the common ground. Remember, we are looking to build consensus.

As an example, you could supply all of the experts with a consolidated list of the responses to our first question on educational change and development and ask them to rank these and explain their ranking decisions. You could also use this stage to ask the panel to identify just one "wildcard" that they think could be a disruptor.

Step 6: Round Three Questions

The final questionnaire aims to focus on supporting decision-making. Hone in on the areas of agreement. What is it the experts are all agreed on? In our example, we may gather feedback on the top five issues identified and ask if they are aligned with these.

(You may wish to have more than three rounds of questioning to reach a closer consensus.)

The trouble is the processes used can lead to a great many trends and patterns making the list of issues to be considered. These need to be prioritized. Here is a tool for this work of prioritization.

Tool 8: Mapping Parallel Trends

Another approach to looking at trends and patterns is to explore the way in which the team is thinking about the future graphically. Think of two dimensions: the vertical axis refers to the extent of change likely to occur over the next 10 years; the horizontal axis refers to the passage of time. In the space between these two dimensions we plot (as if they were graph lines) the trends we are likely to see.

Let us use an example. Think about the future of schools in England between 2015 and 2025, knowing that, for the next five years, the Conservative government intends to pursue the same policies as it did over the previous five. We can ask:

- What is likely to be the level of per capita investment in education at the secondary school?
- Will there be more or less privatization of secondary schools?
- Will teacher-pay rise or fall over this time?
- Will the ratio of classroom teachers to administrators in the system change?
- Will parents have to pay more or less for their child's education?
- Will class sizes go up or down?

- Will there be more or less technology?

– for each question, we can draw a trend line (up means more, down means less) and we draw them all in the same two-dimensional space so that we can see the interaction between them. The result might look something like this:

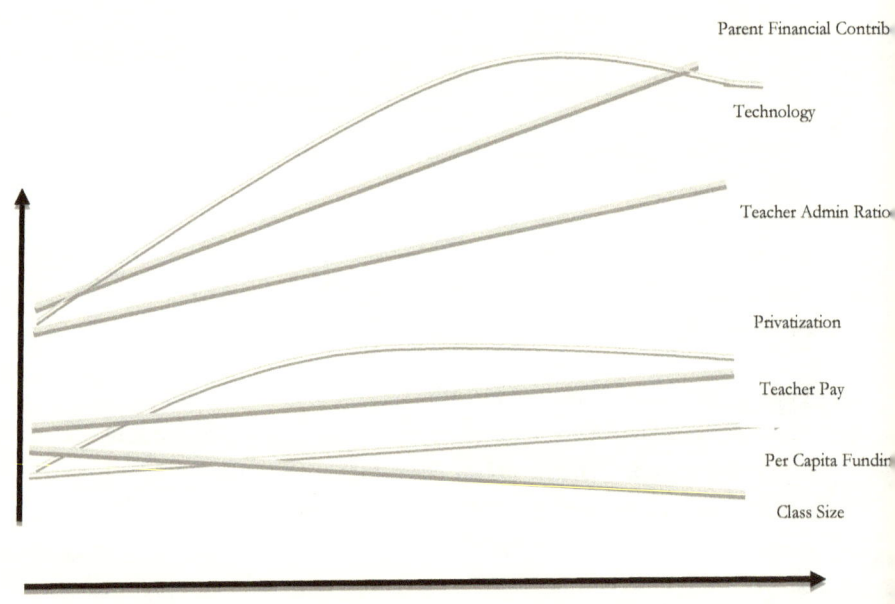

Parent Financial Contrib

Technology

Teacher Admin Ratio

Privatization

Teacher Pay

Per Capita Funding

Class Size

Figure 13: Multiple Patterns on the Same Graph

This visual then becomes a way of backcasting – looking at the 10-year period and working back to the present so that we can understand how these patterns interact.

Tool 9: Prioritization Matrix

What we need to know is what is important and actionable – a trend (demography, for example) may be very important but there is little we can do to influence this trend. The idea here is to look at each trend / pattern we have identified and weight them by attaching a score on a specific criteria (we normally use a score of 0-50 where 50 is high).

The criteria we assess the issues by can vary, but we normally use:

138

- How important is this trend/ pattern to us?
- To what extent can we take action to influence this trend or pattern?
- How difficult will it be to have an impact on this trend/ pattern?

A prioritization matrix looks like this – we show just two trend lines, but there could be any number:

Prioritization Criteria				
Trend / Pattern	Importance (Score 0-50)	Influence (Score 0-50)	Difficulty (Score 0-50)	Total Score
Trend/Pattern 1				
Trend 2				

Step 4: Building Scenarios

Chapter 6 outlines the ideas behind scenario-building and the process by which scenarios are constructed. It also provides an example of a scenario framework – Commerce 2020 – to illustrate this work in action. Lots of scenario examples can be found in a simple Google search and there are helpful web based tools to support this work[40].

We remind you of McKinsey's suggested rules[41]:

1. Always develop and articulate at least four scenarios.
2. Always describe the signposts and warning signals for each scenario.
3. Always name scenarios with simple, yet memorable ("catchy") names so that they can get used frequently in conversation.
4. Never focus a scenario on a single variable (e.g. growth versus decline) – ensure that the scenarios reflect the complexity of the issues at hand.
5. Classify the developed scenarios into preferred, probable, possible, plausible.

But there are three tools we think could be helpful.

Tool 10: Scenario Narratives

This is a simple tool. For each scenario, write a newspaper story as if it were 10, 20 or 30 years from now and the specific scenario had played out in its full glory. It need not be long (the typical opinion piece is between 750 and 800 words) but needs to embrace all of the key elements of the scenario and their impacts. Capture these as graphically and creatively as you can. The idea is to bring these scenarios to life. A similar approach to this same work is to draw a timeline showing key events related to this scenario over a 10-20 year period – what happens when?

(See also our observations in Chapter 7 about other forms of narratives)

Tool 11: Indicators Matrix

How will we know which of the scenarios you have developed is in play? What indicators do you need to track so as to know which scenario is dominant?

We suggest you build a simple set of indicators which would tell you what to look for – here is a way of showing these visually:

Scenario 1 Indicators	Scenario 2 Indicators
1. 2. 3.	1. 2. 3.
Scenario 3 Indicators	**Scenario 4 Indicators**
1. 2. 3.	1. 2. 3.

Tool 12: Uncertainty Matrix

All scenarios contain degrees of uncertainty. We do need to understand the uncertainties involved, especially if we are moving from scenarios to strategic planning based on them. Again we can use a simple tool to capture our understanding of the uncertainties for each of our scenarios:

Scenario	Level of Uncertainty (1-5 Scale)	Impact of Uncertainty (1-5 Scale)	OPTIONS		
			Indicators Needed	Monitoring Activity Required	Action to Reduce Uncertainty
Scenario 1					
Scenario 2					
Scenario 3					
Scenario 4					

Under 'options', we need to include:

- Specific indicators we need to track
- Additional monitoring we need to undertake
- A summary of the actions we intend to undertake (other than monitoring and tracking) to reduce the uncertainty and risk *if* this is important to us.

The purpose of the tool is to better understand the risks associated with a specific scenario.

Step 5: Getting to Strategy

Chapter 8 outlines a systematic approach to strategy development based on both Michael Porter's strategic framework and the idea of strategy as simple rules. There are a great many tools to support strategy formulation and development – just search for such tools as The Five Bold Steps or Strategy Matrix. One we have used a lot is a tool which captures strategy on a single page using a framework of the Strategic House. Here is what this looks like:

Vision:

Mission:

Strategic Imperatives				
2-3 Year Challenges	People	Resources	Processes	Partnerships:
Mantra for the Strategy				
Our People will Have These Qualities	Get:	Feel:	I Am:	
Strategic Foundation	Competences:	Technical Skills:	Enablers:	
All Built On				

What we are trying to do is capture complex strategy in a simple visual. Here is an example – the strategy for an integrated resource centre for data and information for the Government of Alberta – something we worked on in 2005.

Vision: Quality Information About Alberta Available to Anyone, Anywhere at Anytime

Mission: To provide quality data and analysis to support evidence based understanding of the **issues and opportunities in Alberta**

Strategic Imperatives	Creating the platform, tools and processes for access to quality data and analysis to meet demand			
2-3 Year Challenges	**People:** - Build trust and confidence in the people - Encourage and enable co-operation, sharing and peer review - Develop standards to ensure quality and confidence	**Resources** - Simplify access to data / analysis in a one stop shop - Least cost provider of quality data and analysis – first choice - Share the costs	**Processes** - Effective access, search and navigation - Standards based protocols - Efficient purchase - Co-operative management and development	**Partnerships:** - Outstanding service through partnerships - Start within Government, move out over time - Foster strong links across Government

Mantra for the Strategy	SMART – VALUABLE – EFFICIENT – COLLABORATIVE - NIMBLE		
Our People will Have These Qualities	**Get**: *business clarity, efficiency, teamwork, stakeholder alignment and great role models – all at the highest level*	**Feel**: *enabled, empowered, engaged and listened to*	**I Am**: connected, empowered, focused, engaged, creative, involved
Strategic Foundation	**Competencies:** Imagining the possibilities, quality use of data and analysis resources, creativity, connected through virtual teams, in control of processes	**Technical Skills:** Managing knowledge, clear business processes which are well documented, focused outcome and impact measures	**Enablers**: Leadership, partnerships, standards, effective governance, futures-thinking, best practices from around the world
All Built On	FOCUS – INTEGRITY – COMMITMENT – TRUST – QUALITY – STEWARDSHIP – RESULTS		

This strategy led to the creation of a central statistical and analysis team and appropriate web-based tools for this work.

Step 6: Visualizing and Experiencing the Future

Chapter 7 provides a great many examples of how to use tools of visualization, news generation, video and other resources to capture the future. For example, Al Gore's film *An Inconvenient Truth* was his attempt to do precisely this.

There are a great many visualization tools available. The best collection of these can be found at this site: http://www.creativebloq.com/design-tools/data-visualization-712402 and we strongly recommend that you explore these.

Step 7: Living Your Vision in Action

This is about moving from big picture thinking – foresight and strategy – to actually doing the work: action. How do we translate strategy into action?

Tool 13: SiRS

We developed this tool in the early 1990s and have used it ever since. It asks teams at all levels of the organization, having understood strategy, to identify the responses to these seemingly simple questions:

What can we?:

1. STOP doing, because it gets in the way of high performance?

2. IMPROVE—identify something that you do well right now, but need to improve upon so that you can become outstanding.

3. REDESIGN—identify something that you do badly at the moment, but must really rethink because it is essential to becoming a high performing organization.

4. START—identify key things that you don't do now, but better START to do if you have any serious desire of becoming a high-performing organization?

We also want to explore these questions at three different levels. First, ask the participants to answer these questions for themselves—What Can I Stop, Improve, Redesign and Start? Second, at the level of their natural work team ask the participants to answer the questions as a team, What can We Stop, Improve, Redesign and Start? Finally, thinking of the organization as a whole, ask the participants to identify, What the Organization could best Stop, Improve, Redesign, and Start?

A worksheet for this work looks like this:

	STOP	IMPROVE	REDESIGN	START
I can...				
My Team Can				

As an organization, we can…

Some have difficulty understanding the difference between "improve" and "redesign". Our explanation is simple – improve tweaks what we already do, redesign takes us back to the drawing board so that we do process re-engineering for this work.

Our experience is that this tool – simple though it is – is very powerful. When we suggest additional rules (e.g. you can't start something until you stop something or you can't have entries in the "organization" row without putting something in the "I can.." row, we get into a great many issues associated with translating strategy into action.

Tool 14: SMART Action Plans

The other tool – taking SiRS to the next level is to take each item in the SiRS chart and making a SMART plan for this action (once we are all aligned that it is appropriate). SMART refers to:

- Specific actions – what do I want to measure?
- Measurable – how am I going to measure it?
- Attainable – how reasonable is this action and related measures?
- Results focused – will achieving this get us closer to delivering on the strategy?
- Time-based – exactly when will this action achieve the results we need?

We also like to add a statement of who is accountable for achieving these SMART goals into the action plan.

Conclusion

These are the tools we have used in this work. This backpack is not meant to be a definitive collection of such tools – merely a "starter kit" to get you started in this work of engaging in a strategic foresight expedition.

Notes and References

Chapter 1

[1] Denrell, J. and Fang, C. (2010) Predicting the Next Big Thing – Success as a Signal of Poor Judgment. *Management Science*, Volume 56(10), pages 1653-1657.

[2] Tetlock, P. E (2006) *Expert Political Judgment – How Good is It? How Can we Know? New Jersey:* Princeton University Press.

[3] Kahneman, D. (2011) *Thinking Fast and Slow.* Toronto: Doubleday Canada

[4] Reinhart, C. and Rogoff, K. (2013) *This Time Its Different – Eight Centuries of Financial Folly.* New Jersey: Princeton University Press.

[5] See Janis, Irving L. (1982). Groupthink: *Psychological Studies of Policy Decisions and Fiascoes.* Second Edition. New York: Houghton Mifflin.

[6] It has been suggested that those who deny climate change is caused by human activity should be put to death. See http://joannenova.com.au/2012/12/death-threats-anyone-austrian-prof-global-warming-deniers-should-be-sentenced-to-death

[7] Taleb, N. (2010) *The Black Swan – The Impact of the Highly Improbable.* New York: Random House.

[8] For more information, see Wallace, J.W. and Hobbs, P.V (2006) *Atmospheric Science – An Introductory Survey, 2nd Edition.* London: Academic Press.

Chapter 2

[9] See The Economist (2013) The Cost del Sol – Sustainable Energy Meets Unsustainable Costs. July 20th (print edition).

[10] For more information about the 7S's see this description http://en.wikipedia.org/wiki/McKinsey_7S_Framework

[11] Tools to support this are available at http://www.grove.com/S-P-O-T-Matrix

[12] For a description, see http://www.slideshare.net/tetradian/intro-toscore-v1

[13] Porter, M.E. (1996) What is Strategy? *Harvard Business Review*, Nov-Dec, pages 61-78. Reprint 96608.

[14] Eisenhardt, K.M. and Sull, D.N. (2001) Strategy as Simple Rules. *Harvard Business Review*, pages 107-116. Reprint R0101G.

[15] See, for example, Albrecht, Karl and Zemke, R. (1990) *Service America: Doing Business in the New Economy*, New York: Grand Central Publishing.

Chapter 4

[16] Porter, M.E. (1980) *Competitive Strategy*. New York: Free Press.

[17] De Bono, E. (1985) *Six Thinking Hats – An Essential Approach to Business Management*. New York: Little Brown & Co

[18] For a description of this approach, see http://www.isixsigma.com/new-to-six-sigma/getting-started/are-you-ready-how-conduct-maturity-assessment/

[19] The story of Periscope at https://gse-ldt.stanford.edu/students/ma-projects/periscope-story-beneath-surface

[20] This info graphic shows the state of the e-learning industry in 2013: http://www.learndash.com/state-of-the-e-learning-industry-infographic/

Chapter 5

[21] Murgatroyd, S. (2011) *Rethinking the Future – Six Patterns Shaping the New Renaissance*. Edmonton: futureTHINK Press.

[22] Gore, A. (2013) *The Future – Six Drivers of Global Change*. New York: Random House.

[23] Senge, P. (1990) *The Fifth Discipline – The Art and Practice of the Learning Organization*. New York: Doubleday.

[24] For example, see Meyer, M. & Zucker, L. (1998) *Permanently Failing Organizations*. Newbury Park, CA: Sage and also Rouleau, L., Gagnon, S. & Clouter, C. (2008) Revisiting permanently-failing organizations — A practice perspective, *Les Cahiers de Recherche du GePS* 2(1), pp. 17–29.

[25] Tully, J. and Murgatroyd, S. (2013) *Rethinking Post Secondary Education*. Edmonton: futureTHINK Press.

[26] Porter, M.E. (1980) Competitive Strategy. New York: Free Press.

[27] See Hilbert, M., Miles, I. and Othmer, J. (2009) Foresight Tools for Participative Policy Making in Intergovernmental Processes in Developing Countries. *Technological Forecasting and Social Change*, Volume 15(2), pages 880-896.

[28] In establishing the IPCC (see http://www.ipcc.ch/docs/UNGA43-53.pdf) a strong emphasis was given to human induced climate change.

Chapter 6

[29] Roxburgh, C. (2009) The Use and Abuses of Scenarios. See www.mckinsey.com/insights/strategy/the_use_and_abuse_of_scenarios

[30] ibid

[31] Meitzner, D. and Reger, G. (2005) Advantages and Disadvantages of Scenario Approaches for Strategic Foresight. *International Journal of Technology Intelligence and Planning*, Volume 1(2), pages 220-239.

[32] Mills, A.J. and Murgatroyd, S. J. (1991) *Organizational Rules – A Framework for Understanding Organizational Action*. Milton Keynes: Open University Press.

Chapter 7

[33] There is a good collection of such visualizations at http://emergentbydesign.com/2012/10/18/12-trend-maps-visualizations-future-2/

[34] Levine, R., Schelling, T. and Jones, W. (1991) *Crisis Games Twenty-Seven Years Later*. Santa Monica, CA: Rand Corporation (mimeo).

Chapter 8

[35] Murgatroyd, S. and Morgan, C. (1993) *Total Quality Management and The School*. Milton Keynes: Open University Press.

[36] See also Morgan, C. and Murgatroyd, S. (1994) *Total Quality Management and the Public Sector*. Milton Keynes: Open University Press.

[37] Murgatroyd, S. and Morgan, C. (1993) op cit.

[38] Eisenhardt, K.M. and Sull, D. (2001) Strategy as Simple Rules. Harvard Business Review, January pages 107-116.

[39] Porter, M.E. (1996) What is Strategy? *Harvard Business Review*, Nov-Dec pages 61-78. Reprint 96608.

Backpack and Tool Kit

[40] See The Scenario Tool Kit at http://scentools.sourceforge.net/

[41] See Roxburgh, C. (2009) The Use and Abuses of Scenarios. See www.mckinsey.com/insights/strategy/the_use_and_abuse_of_scenarios

www.ingramcontent.com/pod-product-compliance
Lightning Source LLC
Chambersburg PA
CBHW032022170526
45157CB00002B/817